FROM PRISON TO PRAISE

Stephen O. Howard

thank you.
may this book bless you

Stephen Howard

FROM PRISON
TO PRAISE

Stephen O. Howard

T&J Publishers
A Small Independent Publisher
with a Big Voice

Printed in the United States of America by
T&J Publishers (Atlanta, GA.)
www.TandJPublishers.com

All Bible verses used are from the King James Version
(1982) by Thomas Nelson, Inc.,

Cover design by Timothy Flemming, Jr. (T&J Publishers)
Book format and layout by Timothy Flemming, Jr. (T&J
Publishers)

ISBN: 978-0-692-68627-0

To contact author, go to:
http://www.sohoward.com
info@sohoward.com
Twitter: Stephen O. Howard

DEDICATIONS

First, I want to give thanks to God, my Father; and to the Lord, Jesus the Christ, for saving me and giving me another chance in life. Thank you, Lord, for keeping Your promise!

I also want to thank my mom, my dad, and all of my siblings. You were instrumental in shaping me into the person I am today!

To my son Stephen, thank you for believing in me even during my time of addiction and imprisonment!

To all of my sons and daughters (Corey, Richard, Rahkem, ConQhetta, Reshina, Brittany and Nedra) thank you for allowing me to love your mother and be a part of your lives!

To all 18 of my grandchildren, you are Paw Paw's gifts!

My Bishop, Eusebio D. Phelps, and First Lady Laurona Phelps, thank you for seeing God in me and pushing me to my greatness!

To the members of my church, True Visions Global Christian Ministry, THE BEST CHURCH IN THE CITY OF DECATUR, YOU ROCK!

Thank you to my publisher, T&J Publishers, and to all others who assisted in publishing my first book.

To Bianca Williams, who also helped me with this book,

you're the bomb, girl! I love you so much!

To all of my readers, I hope and pray that my life's story blesses your heart, and know that if God did it for me, He can do it for you!

Last, but not least, to my best friend, my first girlfriend, the love of my life, and now my wife, Latasha Renee Howard, thank you for believing in me. It is because of you I am who I am today. Love you, baby!

"The righteous cry, and the LORD heareth, and delivereth them out of all their troubles."
—*Psalm 34:17*

TABLE OF CONTENTS

INTRODUCTION:
A WALKING MIRACLE

SOMETIMES I WONDER TO MYSELF HOW AM I STILL alive. It still amazes me to this very day. Out of all that I have been through, it would be impossible for me to count the number of times I should have died and become just another statistic. I am a walking miracle. I am a living testament to the power and saving grace of God. I am an example of why you should never give up on yourself or those you love. I am proof that there is no prison, whether mental, physical or spiritual, that you or your loved one can't come out of. Christ has provided for us a way of escape from the darkness in our lives. Even if you are in a physical prison (which I spent the majority of my life in) and are facing no chance of getting out, just know that if you place your life in the hands of Christ He will do the miraculous in and through your life. With God, all things are possible.

This book is about my life. It shows how God was able to break the chains of addiction in my life and bring me out of a pit of destruction. It wasn't easy. I'll admit that. It took a lot of time and a lot of prayer from my loved ones to pull me through. But I came through...and so can you. And when God pulled me through, it was done in such a way that no one could deny the existence of God.

The good thing about Jesus the Christ is He is a living Savior. He is alive today. He still performs miracles today. He still delivers. He still heals. He does the same things today that He did over two thousand years ago. I experienced this miracle working power in my own life first hand. That is why the Bible tells us to give God a try and put Him to the test. Christianity is filled with supernatural miracles, signs and wonders, and Christ's promise to us is that He will perform them in our lives if and when we call upon Him...just to prove to the world that He is the true and living God.

It doesn't matter how long it takes. Never give up. Never give up on God. Never throw down your faith. Never stop believing for your miracle and your break-through. As you will see in the pages of this book, if you hold on to your faith in Jesus Christ and truly turn to Him in everything and for everything, He will answer and change your life . . . forever.

Chapter 1:
THE BEGINNING

There I was, sitting on a hard steel bunk whose mattress was as thin as sheet metal and whose pillow resembled a flimsy thin pancake sitting on a cold, unloved plate - some people may call this torture. Nightly, those of us in this facility slept on these "beds", if you can call them that. As I sat in my cell, my mind reflected back to the role that I played which led to me becoming a prisoner both in my own mind as well as in the Georgia Penal Institution.

Hold up! Wait a minute. I think I'm getting ahead of myself. Let me rewind and go back to the beginning, to the time before my incarceration and help you to understand what events transpired in my life that landed me in such a place and ultimately led to me writing this book.

I WAS BORN DECEMBER 30TH, 1967 TO WILLIE PAUL Howard, Sr. and Lovillar Howard. Every since I was born, people had been telling me that I was special. Out of all of my siblings, I was born identical to my father. My mom told me that when the nurse brought me out of the womb, my eyes were already open and I was just looking all around. The nurse then said, "Oh my God, please call me when he grows up. God got a calling on his life and I want to witness it!"

My mother and father kept us in church every Sunday. Sometimes, we would go to church Monday through Saturday on top of having to get up early Sunday morning to go to church. We stayed in church constantly! I know that Bible says in Proverbs 22:6 to "Train up a child in the way he should go, And even when he is old he will not depart from it," but to me, this was a bit overboard. My parents were so strict about church that they even made me go once with no shoes on. I lost my shoes one day and my mother told me, "If you don't find your shoes, you are going without them!" I couldn't find them, and she made me go to church without them. I sat on the second row where I could better hide my feet due to the embarrassment I felt.

I came up in a decent household. My parents were very much in love, and they truly loved us, their kids—all 12 of us. They raised us how be respectable young men and women. We were taught good manners, alongside the Christian faith. But although I knew of Jesus and God, I didn't actually have a personal intimate relationship with Him. I would come to discover that there are some things your parents can't give you later on in my life. Growing up, I usually got whatever I wanted. Usually, all I had to do was ask for what I wanted and I got it; sometimes, I would act out to have my way. Of course, there were times when I didn't get my way. I remember one incident when I went over to our church's youth leader's house to spend the night, something I would do almost every weekend. But this particularly day, Calvin, the youth leader, took me to McDonald's, and then afterwards, we went to Richway department store. While there, I saw some action figures that I wanted. "Calvin, can I have that Stretch Armstrong?" I asked.

"I ain't got no money to get that doll, boy," Calvin replied.

I poked my bottom lip out so far you could have sat a drinking glass on it. When we got back to the car, I threw a temper tantrum and tossed my milkshake and French Fries all over the car. Talk about getting a butt whipping! I got my butt torn up that day, and I never did that again!

Growing up, everything seemed pretty routine: go to school, do school work, get good grades, go home, get ready to go to church, go to church, go home, sleep, wake-up and do it all over again the next day. In our home growing up, we didn't own a television. The only form of entertainment we had was the Bible and other educational books. I had little to no idea that life outside of church existed. Everything—and I mean, everything—I knew revolved around church. When it came to school, I was very shy; at least, all the way up until my sophomore year.

In elementary school, I didn't know how to communicate and interact well with other kids, so I basically stayed to myself. Some people would say I was antisocial. There was one girl in school I had my eyes on, but I was too terrified to speak to her. Every year we would end up in the same home room class—and in most of the other classes together—but she never knew that I liked her.

She probably didn't even know that I existed, let alone liked her.

Growing up, I was the typical momma's boy. I truly loved my momma! My sister, Grace, and I were the youngest in the family, and we went everywhere our mother went. I clung to the hem of my momma's dress like the woman with the issue of blood in the Bible who desperately clung to the hem of Jesus' garment. Everywhere I would go with my mother I would hear the same things: "Oh, he's such a handsome boy! Oh, he's so adorable!" Often times, after we'd leave a place, momma would ask me, "Stephen, what did that lady say about you?"

I would usually say, "She said I look gooood!" with my little head blown up. I can honestly confess that I was a spoiled momma's boy. I enjoyed being so.

My father was a bishop in the church. He took the ministry very seriously. He hated to be late for church. He hated to be late, period, regardless of where we were going. He was a very punctual man, a very disciplined person. On Sunday morning's, my father would get up early and go around the house waking everyone up. I can still hear his voice now: "JD, Steve Sugarmeat, Grace, get up and get ready for church!!" None of us had a choice of whether or not we'd get up and go to church either. If you lived on 433 Ashburton Ave SE in Atlanta, Georgia, you were going to church—there were no if's, and's, or but's about it. Father would make sure we were all up and ready, and he never let us leave the house without a good breakfast in our stomaches.

At this time in my life, I really was happy going to church—I actually enjoyed being there all of the time. I enjoyed singing the church songs and watching my brothers play the piano and drums. As I would watch my father preach, the thought would resonate on the inside of me that I was going to be a preacher just like him. There was enough going on in the church to keep my attention, but there was also something else that kept me interested in church: the girls. There were benefits to being the preacher's son. All of the girls at church loved the musicians and the preachers, and because I was the preacher's son—the bishop's youngest son at that—all of the little girls had their eyes set on me. But I had my eyes set on one girl: her name was Latasha. Back then, Latasha was known by a certain nickname: Tot. She was, to me, the prettiest little thing in our church, and I anxiously wanted her to be my little girlfriend. It was interesting that at church, I wasn't shy like I was at school. Perhaps, that was because church was such a place of familiarity and comfort for me, a place where I was more known and accepted. I felt free to be open there.

My father drove a sky blue station wagon. On Sundays after church, all of the children wanted to come over to our house to play. The good thing is Tot and Grace were best friends—this gave Tot an advantage over all the other little girls, and this also meant I would be privileged to see Tot...a lot. After church, Tot would hop into our car to come over to our house almost every Sunday. When she would come to the car to get in, I always made sure I had a seat waiting for her right next to me. I thought I was smooth. Even back then, I thought I was a ladies' man.

When Tot got in the car, she would sit next to me and I would ease my little arms behind her; she would then scoot over little closer to me. We both were, as the old folks used to say, "Just mannish."

When we would get home from church, momma and daddy would always go into their bedroom to rest before dinner, and the rest of us would go and change clothes and then rush outside to play; and at other times, Grace would take Latasha into her bedroom to play. I would always try to get Tot to come upstairs to my bedroom, instead . . . that is, until Grace would tattle on me by calling Momma and saying, "Momma, tell Steve to leave us alone! He trying to get us to come up stairs!"

"Grace, you make me sick!" I'd say to myself. Because of her, I could never get Tot to my bedroom. But my luck was about to soon change.

One Sunday, I got a chance to be alone with Latasha. We finally alone, outside, standing behind a car. That's when we kissed! "Oh, I'm the man now!" I thought. I kissed my dream girl! You couldn't tell me anything after that.

Our junior church leader, Calvin Bennett, spoiled me rotten. He gave me everything I asked for, and all the other boys in church hated me because of that. I had the sharpest suits for Easter and all the latest toys for Christmas. Money wasn't an issue for me, either. The only thing I had to do was go to Calvin and utter the words "I want it . . ." and I had it. I was used to getting whatever I wanted. I knew how to play on people's emotions and get my way. And now, I have the best girl in church. I was in heaven.

As I got older, all of my time was spent in church and my social life became more and more nonexistent, especially in school. For a long time, I didn't participate in any activities outside of the church, but at the same time, I was beginning to come out of my shell of shyness. I was around the age of 13 when me and a friend of mine would meet up on the side of our middle school and smoke weed—some people call it a joint; others call it by its more commonly known name: Marijuana. We would smoke weed and then go to class. Little did I know at the time that the weed would lead me down the path of destruction, nearly destroying my life and the lives of countless others along the way. One particular day around this time, I remember being in my room with my older sister and another relative who was older than me, and we were *smoking our backs out* (for those of you that don't know what that means, *smoking your back out* means "smoking without taking a break"). I was soooooo high! I can remember going down into the kitchen afterwards and raiding the refrigerator with an insatiable appetite. I wanted to eat everything I set my eyes on. The whole time I was doing this, I couldn't stop giggling and laughing. I remember standing by the kitchen sink and laughing so hard while bending over that my head went into the sink which was filled with nasty dishwater and all. When I pulled my head up out of the water, I was still laughing and acting crazy. Unfortunately, from that time moving forward, I began to spiral downhill into an addiction that turned my life completely up-side-down. I started using drugs for a number of reasons, but there was one reason that I didn't talk much about. As a child, I experienced the pain of being violated by another, much older girl. And even though my father caught her and punished her for it, I still suffered with the pain and the trauma of that event. At first, I thought that by using drugs I would be able to suppress the emotional hurt, and perhaps, even erase the memory of what I had experienced as a child. I decided that drugs would not only become my adventure, my door to a world I had not experienced before, but they would also become my safe haven, my way of escape from the emotional pain that rested at the core of my soul, a pain I didn't talk much about.

CHAPTER 2:
THE ADDICTION

There I was, standing in a hotel room, me and everyone else armed like we were getting ready to go to war. Some of the guys had automatic weapons; others had shot guns—you name it, we had it. And there she was in the middle of us all with a suitcase full of money and Coke like a quarterback in the middle of a huddle. Our mission was to take over Atlanta. I idolized Tony Montana from the movie Scarface. I wanted to be just like him. How did I get this far gone?

GROWING UP, I ALWAYS CONSIDERED MYSELF TO be the ladies man—you could call me Mr. Romeo. It became my ambition in life to be on television—that is, after we finally got one. I wanted to be a professional singer, be in the movies—whatever it took to get women's attention. I wanted every girl I placed my eyes on. I was growing into a womanizer. I went to Barbizon School of Modeling because I figured this would open doors for me to reach my goals of getting famous and getting girls.

I was around 17 years old when I started modeling for the Bronner Brothers hair shows; I also modeled clothes for Tony Dorsey. I quickly discovered, however, that in this world anything goes—and I do mean anything. For example, one day, during a photo shoot, one of the guys came to me and said that he needed to fix my clothes, but I figured he had something else on his mind other than my clothes. He tried to reach down into my pants, claiming that he needed to straighten my tool for the camera. Immediately, I hollered, "HOLD UP!!!! I got it!!" When he went into the other room to get some supplies, like Sweet Brown said, "I RAN FOR MY LIFE!"

I modeled for a while. I began to develop a love of the runway, that is until one of my siblings, Angela (who we called Sugarmeat), came home one particular day. "Step," she said (that's what she use to call me. "Step" was short for "Stephen"). "I know this Cuban woman that love black men. She got a lot of money and all the coke you want. If you take me over there, I promise you she'll like you."

"OK. What's her name?" I asked.

"Miss B," she responded.

"OK. Let's go," I responded.

At that time, I had no money, not even for gas. And even though I had never seen or used cocaine, I saw this as my opportunity to get paid and laid at the same time. So, out the door we went; and before we knew it, we were at Miss B's door. (Knock, Knock, Knock)

"Who is it?" Miss B asked.

"It's me, B," Angela responded. Miss B then opened the door and let us into her apartment. When I walked in my attention was immediately drawn to my left. I was startled by what I saw. I had never seen that much white powder (cocaine) in my life. The dining room table was covered with Coke, a scale to weigh it, and bags to put it in.

"B, this my uncle, Steve. He's cool, and he got a car," said Angela.

"Hey," said Miss B, looking at me.

"Hello," I responded.

I looked to my right and spotted a sofa and then headed that way. As I was taking my seat, the phone began to ring. Miss B answered the phone and started discussing something in Spanish. Once she hung up the phone, she said, "I need a ride."

"My uncle got a car," said Angela.

Miss B looked at me and asked the million dollar question: "Do you have a car?"

"Yes," I replied

"If you give me a ride, I'll pay you," she said. Not knowing what I was getting myself into—what I was about to transport—I took her across town where she made a drug deal. When she finished, she returned to the car and placed $50.00 in my hand. From that moment on, I was sold. I earned an additional $300.00 more that day just driving her back and forth to make these deals.

Miss B shared with me one day why she tended to move around a lot, why she moved to another apartment community from a previous one: she said she had a habit of using drugs and she didn't trust herself. So, on moving day, she came to me and handed me a kilo of coke and said, "I need you to take this to the apartment and hide it from me. I don't trust myself because I keep going in it, and we need to make money." I was so green at this point, knowing nothing about where to hide drugs. I knew very little about coke, let alone where to hide it; but I had to try. So, in the new apartment, I searched for a hiding spot. I finally found one: it was over the refrigerator, in the AC vent. I continued to secure the package; and after I had finished, there was a knock on the door.

"Who is it?" I asked.

"Sugarmeat!" I opened the door and Angela came in. "I got somebody who want to buy that 'ki'. I told B and she said, 'OK. Come and get it from you.'" (Keep in mind that I was very ignorant about the drug game at this point.) So, instead of me calling Miss B, I went along with Sugarmeat's word. I then went to the hiding spot where I stashed the drugs and retrieved them and gave them to her; and out the door she went. If I had known better, I would have went with Angela. I don't know. Perhaps, by making better decisions at that point, I could have prevented the hell we were all about to go through.

About 30-45 minutes after I gave Angela the drugs and she left the apartment, both she and Miss B came into the apartment. But I noticed that Angela was crying. "What's wrong?" I asked.

"She got robbed," Miss B said.

"How? What happened? Who it was? What kind of car he drove?" I asked. Maybe I was just a little slow or ignorant, but I even I knew we were all in deep trouble; I could sense it. I knew the Cubans didn't play when it came to their products. I had seen the movie Scarface enough times to know that you didn't mess with their dope.

"So, what are we going to do?" I asked Miss B.

"Let me make a call," she responded. After she made the call, she said, "They want their money! They don't believe me!" By this time, my heart began to beat super fast. Now I knew beyond a shadow of a doubt that we were in serious trouble.

"What we gonna do?!" I asked.

"Run!!" That was all Miss B said. So, we all packed up and ran. (It's better to be on the run from the police than a drug lord.) We packed up and moved to the other side of the town, hoping that we would be safe until coming up with the money—$45,000 to be exact. We moved to the west side of Atlanta and started selling drugs over there.

Talk about problems? We ran into all kind of trouble: trouble from the maintenance man threatening to tell the police on us if we didn't pay him to "play", to one of our guys shooting his gun off in the house and the bullet going through the wall and grazing a mother's arm as she held her baby. We experienced trouble, trouble, trouble. And to top things off, we found out that OC had put a bounty of $10,000 out on our heads. Now we were truly hiding out.

One day, Miss B and I went to get something to eat. We decided to walk to KFC so we could talk alone. We needed to come up with a plan on how to get the money we owed OC. On our way home, we heard a car approaching us from behind. We turned around. It was OC. When the car stopped, OC looked at her and said, "Get in the car." As we got in the car, Miss B got behind OC. She looked at me and asked for my gun. When I gave it to her, she move forward and place the gun in the back of the seat that OC was sitting in. They began discussing something in Spanish. I later learned that he was telling her that he had a grenade in his pocket, and she was telling him that she had a gun aimed in the center of his back.

When we got back to the apartment, we all went into the dining room and sat down at the dining room table. OC asked for a plate and poured an ounce of coke on it. He looked at me, motioning for me to get some. "NO!!!" shouted Miss B. She then told me to go to the back with her sons while she discussed the matter with OC. Back in the bedroom, there was a guy and a girl—I never knew their names. They were back in the bedroom *cutting out windowpane* (i.e. doing Acid). Acid is a drug that causes you to hallucinate. Some people lose their minds after using it. Thank God that drug never entered into my body. About 30 minutes later, Miss B called me back into the dining room. OC was gone and we had a "ki" and a half of coke.

OC told her everything. As it turned out, my sister's boyfriend snitched on us to OC because he wanted that $10,000 reward OC put out on our heads. (Now, ain't that something.) We ended up moving back to Decatur, Georgia in my old neighborhood, and went right back to work selling drugs as if we had never left. I got in my car and drove around the hood looking for a place to sell my dope. When I came to 3rd Avenue, I knew this was where I wanted to set up shop. Soon afterwards, I started using myself, which violated a golden rule in the drug game: Don't get high on your on supply. At first, I only used a small amount: a hit in the morning to start the day off, then a little more around lunch time, and then a little more before and after dinner. I thought that I would be OK, not realizing that I was on the road to becoming a junkie—I was driving full speed ahead on the road to hell. Cocaine quickly consumed my life. It got to the point that my love for drugs was stronger than my desire for women, my family, and God. While living with Miss B, I discovered that I couldn't trust anyone. Our "family" grew from 10 to 20 young black men looking to make money in the drug game—yes, we considered ourselves a family and we were willing to die for one another, or so I thought. We began making money at all cost.

You have to watch who you allow to get close to you. I believe this is what happened to Miss B. One day, a guy came into the house with her, and I just got this feeling in the pit of my belly that he wasn't right. I don't know if it was the way he dressed, his laugh, or if it was the way he tried to fit in; I just had a bad feeling about him. Miss B came to me and told me that she was going down to Florida and asked if I wanted to go. I asked her who all was going. She replied, "Me, you, and Butch." When she said he (Butch) was going, I was like 'Hell naw! I ain't going nowhere with this dude.' So, they left and went to Florida together. I haven't seen or heard from Miss B since. The last I heard was that she was caught trafficking 30 kilos back to Atlanta and the Feds got her. Ain't that something?

There I was, wondering what my next move was going to be. I didn't want to move back home with momma and daddy. I didn't save any money. I still had my car, which probably wasn't such a good thing to be honest, looking back. What in the heck am I going to do? I wondered to myself. On top of these concerns, I was also stuck with a drug habit, and I didn't know where to turn for help. I ended up going over to my auntie's house in Summerhill where there were drugs galore. I knew that as long as I stayed around there, I would eventually get some dope and money—I mean, after all, I still had a car. My nephew approached me and asked me to take him to Bankhead Court. Bankhead was known as one of the roughest projects in Atlanta. People got shot and killed just about every day in Bankhead. "For what?" I asked him.

"To buy some break-down dimes. I'll give you one and smoke a primo with you," He said. I didn't know what a primo was, but I did know what a dime was. When he came back to the car, I saw the crack in his hand and my eyes bulged.

"Man, what's that?" I asked.

"This them break-downs," He said. "You got a cigarette?"

"No. I ain't got nothing," I said.

"OK. Stop by the store." He went in and bought some cigarettes, then got back into the car, made a primo, and then fired it up.

"Man, that stank," I said. But as soon as I hit it, it was all over: I was now hook on crack cocaine. I didn't realize it at the time that crack cocaine would turn my life completely upside down. So, there I was in Summerhill smoking crack cocaine. It didn't seem bad at first because seemingly everyone was doing it, but as time progressed I began to get worse. What made matters worse was, during this time, there was a guy by the name of Hollywood—he came into Summerhill; he was a dope dealer. He looked at me and asked me if I wanted to sell drugs. "Hell yeah," I replied.

I thought this was the opportunity to get all the dope that I could smoke. So, he gave me a bag of crack cocaine and asked me for my Social Security Number and my address so that he would know where I stayed and how to find me. But none of that mattered to me then because all I cared about was getting crack cocaine. It never dawned on me that I was placing my parents, my siblings, and everyone else that I love in danger. All I cared about was getting dope.

I sold my soul to the devil for crack cocaine. I began to sell some, smoke some; sell some, smoke some; smoke some; smoke more; sell less, smoke more; smoke more; sell less; sell less; smoke more; smoke all of it; sell none of it . . . . And then, I found myself in deep trouble once again.

There I was, hiding for my life again, afraid to step outside. I didn't know what to do. I would always look over my shoulder when walking down the street. I couldn't go to the store because I was fearful for my life. I lived in a constant state of fear and paranoia. I would go out only at night and stay in the house all day...like a Vampire. I sold my soul and realized it was time for the devil to collect—and I was scared as hell!

But God...

The Bible says God will make a way of escape for you when in trouble. I didn't have a relationship with Christ at that time, but He was still covering, protecting, and keeping watch over me. I thank God I had a praying mother who cried out to the Lord day and night; I know this because every time I looked around I saw Hollywood's car pulling into the driveway of my apartment

complex; he would always ask everyone, "Have you seen Step?" Everyone would always tell him,
  "No, I haven't"
They were looking out for me. I told them if "Hollywood came looking for me, you haven't seen me." This went on for a while. Every morning, I would leave out, trying to find drugs; every evening, I would run into the house to hide; every night, I would leave out, looking over my shoulder.

My auntie called my mother and told her that I was over there in her neighborhood, and every morning when she would go outside, she would witness me running around, trying to get dope. She asked my parents to come and get me. What we didn't know was that the police was across the street surveilling everything that was going on in the apartments. Summerhill was a very hot dope trap and the police were making a case to lock everyone up.

My auntie called my mom and dad to tell them about my activities. My dad immediately hopped in his car and drove over to the neighborhood where he found me and told me to get in the car. I got in the car, and believe it or not, a sigh of relief came over me. A couple of days later, the Atlanta's Red Dogg Drug Force raided those apartments, carrying out a sting operation in Sumerhill which led to the arrests of many in that area. Talk about being spared!

I wasn't home for no more than 30 mins before I was back on the streets, searching for a hit of dope. Oh yeah, I forgot to mention that before my father came and got me, I lost my car. I can't even recall how I lost it. Now that's crazy. I know. That is the type of thing that will happen to you when you're asleep mentally and spiritually. When my dad took me home I was back in the streets smoking, drinking, and looking for ways to get money again. I was shooting bad—and I do mean baaaaad.

There were times when I didn't go home at all because I was too busy looking for that next hit. My habit got to the point that I started neglecting my hygiene. It grew worse and worse. But I knew within my heart that there had to be a better way. My soul was crying out for help. There was a longing in my spirit for relief, but crack had her claws in my soul and it did not want to relinquish its grip. I tried to quit so many times on my own but failed miserably. I walked the streets night and day, crying within and begging God for help. I had problems getting my hands on money, so I came up with a great idea: I decided that if I was to go home I could get some money from my mom and dad. So, I went home with intentions of playing the loving son; I even started going to church. On Sundays, while church was going on, I would go outside and smoke cigarettes and then go back into the church smelling like a Tobacco factory. I cooked up a plan to get money from the saints; so, every time church service was taking place, I was there. I didn't care if it was on a Wednesday, Friday, or Monday; it didn't matter; all that mattered was there was someone there with money in their pockets—or purse. I was determined to be there for that reason alone. There was one mother at the church we called Mother Ross. She always had money. Every night after church service, I would walk her to her car, acting like a total gentleman; but my true motive was to pick her pocket book for drug money. But God has a funny way of doing things. Regardless of how many times I attempted to steal from her, I was never successful. God truly does protect His children.

The 'going to church thing' didn't quite work out the way I had hoped, so I quit going. I decided instead that I would have more success just rambling through momma's purse and daddy's wallet to find money. At first I would try to be slick about it, but as time progressed, my desperation grew so that I began taking every penny I saw, not caring that my stealing was becoming more and more obvious.

"Stephen, did you take my money?" I recall my Dad once asking.

"No, Sir," I lied...like I did every time he confronted me.

"Stephen, did you take money out of my purse?" my mom asked.

"No, momma," I lied. I would lie constantly to my parents.

I thought I was so slick that I would pretend to leave the house and then sneak back in through the back door just to steal some more from my parents, but all the while, I had this sick feeling in the pit of my stomach—as a dope fiend would say, "I got the bubble guts." The crazy thing about the Holy Spirit is that He sees everything you do and will always tell on you—I used to call Him a tattle tale. There were times when I would sneak into my mother's room to steal from her and I just knew that there was no way she could have known that I was there; still, she would call me—"STEVE!!!!!"

"Ma'am!"

"Where's my money, boy?!"

"I ain't got yo money, momma!"

CHAPTER 2: THE ADDICTION

"Yes you do, boy. The Holy Ghost told me you went in my room and got my money! Now, give me my money back right now!"

Despite how much I tried to protest, she knew I had her money. I would feel very ashamed after getting got caught, and find myself quite often reaching into my pocket to pull out her money and hand it to her.

I was around 20 years old now, and I caused my parents to develop a new habit: they had to start hiding their purses and wallets in order to keep their money. After a while, I got to the point where I became tired; I was tired of doing drugs and being in the streets. I wanted to change, so I decided to ask for help. I remember one night after smoking all my money up, I went into my mother's bedroom where she was in bed, and opened up to her: "Momma?"

"Huh?"

"I need help."

"From what?"

"Drugs."

"What, you still using marijuana?"

"No, momma. Crack." She got quite for a minute, and then asked me what we needed to do. "I don't know. I'm just tired, momma. I'm tired."

The next morning, my mother was on the phone seeking help for me. When momma found some help, she called me into her room.

"I found a rehab on Boulevard that will help you if you want it," she proclaimed. But I was operating in denial, being delusional. I figured that morning that since I wasn't high anymore, I didn't need to go anywhere. I figured that I was only talking like that last night because I was high. But since I did open my big mouth and express those things to my mom as if feeling sorry for myself, I went along with her recommendation. We pulled up at the rehab center, and when we went in I started to have second thoughts about it. Man, I don't know if I want to do this, I thought to myself. When my mother told them about my habit and expressed to them that I was seeking out for help, they told her I had to be clean for 24 hours. Now, how do you expect a junkie to be clean for that long? When we left the rehab and got home, I was back off to the race. l was back on the streets, doing dope; but deep within, I was crying out for help. I said to myself, "No, you are not going to die! You are strong! You can do it! You can survive!" I went back home and told momma that I was going to do better. I then went and found a job working for Kroger in Stone mountain, Georgia. I was doing pretty good. I started out as a courtesy clerk and worked my way up to produce. I mean, I was doing gooooood. I had not used drugs in a month. I thought I had my addiction beat, but little did I know that giant was only playing possum, waiting for the perfect opportunity to strike.

CHAPTER 3:
THE WIFE THAT NEVER WAS

ONE DAY, WHILE ON MY WAY TO WORK, I WAS riding the bus when my soon-to-be first wife got on. By this time, I was looking good: I got my weight back; I was socializing. I looked at her and noticed how fine she was. But if I only knew then what I was about to get myself into, I never would have said one word to her. But you know what they say: '*Hind sight is a mugg.*' We were on the bus and she kept looking back at me. The bus was almost at my stop. I realized I needed to gather my courage and introduce myself to her before. "Hey, can I talk to you for a minute?"

"Yeah," she responded.

"So what's your name?" I asked, moving closer to her.

"Connie," she replied.

"Mine's Steve." I got her phone number right before she got off the bus. I called her the next day, but she never answered the phone. During this time, I started using drugs again. The giant inside of me had awaken and he was mad as hell. (I was searching for a release/

excuse and I believed she was it.)

My brother had gotten out of prison (after doing eight years) and came home, but there was one problem though: he was crazy. When he was younger, he was in a band. He could sing! It was told to me that when he'd get up on stage to sing, all of the women would go ballistic. People say he sounded like Maxwell. But one day, after a gig, he went to his table where his friends were and got a drink; he then had to go to the restroom, and while in the restroom, his friends slipped a Mickie in his drink. When my brother came back from the restroom, he took a sip of his drink and it took a serious tole on his mind. Whatever they put in his drink caused him to lose his mind and go crazy. He went up the street some days later and robbed a gas station, which led to him going to prison for eight years; and when he came home, he was not the same. My mother saw to it that my brother received assistance from the State.

On this one particular morning, I wanted some dope, but I didn't have any money. Thinking I was slick, I decided to sneak into my father's room and steal some money while he was asleep. So I went into my parents' bedroom, crawled under their bed, and took about thirty dollars, not knowing that money was my brother's money—my crazy brother's money!!!! When I came out from under the bed and stood up, my brother was standing right there in the room with a large kitchen knife in his hand. He looked at me with murderous eyes. If I ever needed God before, I sure needed him at that moment. My brother looked at me and said, "I'm gonna kill you, mutha f****** a** nigga!"

I was looking at him and thinking, "Oh, hell!

Don't kill me, freaking Jason!" He lunged at me the first time and the knife hit me in my chest. It didn't go deep, but I felt it. When I looked down I noticed blood pouring out of my chest. I looked back up at him and then lunged for the knife. I didn't know that he could move that fast! By the time daddy woke up and got between us, I had been stabbed four times—the most damage was done to my left side just under my arm, two inches from my heart. My dad managed to get him away from me and took him into another room. I ran into the bathroom and looked myself over in the mirror to see where I had been stabbed. When I saw a hole in my side, I placed my right hand over it and tried to prevent the blood from coming out. When I put my hand there, three of my fingers went inside the hole. I then placed my whole hand over the hole to try to prevent the blood from coming out. My sister, Grace, came into the bathroom and asked me to let her see my wounds. When I removed my hand, blood began pouring out, resembling something you'd see in a horror movie. I said to myself, "Oh God!"

I went into the hallway and laid down on the floor on my right side hoping that would prevent the blood from pouring out. By the time the paramedics got to our house, I was going in and out of consciousness. I was rushed to the emergency room at the hospital. My condition was getting worse. When I opened my eyes, I saw the doctor putting stitches in my right wrist. Shocked, I asked, "He got me there, too?" I then lost consciousness again. When I regained consciousness, I saw my family looking at me through a window. My sister, Hannah, was crying. I said to myself, "What's wrong with her?" and then…I lost consciousness again. After I woke up, my mother and the rest of my family was there in the recovery room with me. They didn't tell me until two weeks later that the knife was two inches from my heart. I could have died that day trying to get some drugs. After I got home about five of my female friends came over to visit me. I was dating each of them. When the last "girlfriend" came over to the house, all hell broke loose; they decided they wanted to fuss and fight. I put all of them out. "Get out!" I shouted. "You only want one thing from me, and I only want one thing from you. You know what that is!" As they headed towards the door, each one came over and gave me a kiss and then walked out of the door. I then picked up the phone and called the girl that I met on the bus. She finally answered the phone. I told her what had happened.

"Oh, I'm so sorry to hear that," she responded.

"Can I come see you?"

"Yes," I responded. She came over. That same night I had her in my bed. Wow! When I got with her I did not know that my life was about to make a turn for the worse. I made choices that were not beneficial for anyone. At first, everything was going pretty good. She was the only girl I wanted to spend time with. As time progressed, she became everything to me. I remember the first time we made love: we were upstairs in my father's house in my bedroom. When we finished, my brother came and knocked on the door. I thought my brother was cool and wouldn't tell daddy or momma, but when he came in and saw a white girl in my bed, he instantly ran downstairs to tell daddy I had a white girl upstairs in my bedroom naked.

"Steve!" My dad called. I went downstairs to see

what he wanted. "You got somebody in your room?"

"No sir," I lied.

"Yes you do! JD told me you got some girl upstairs in your room!"

Dad got up and went to the stairs, heading upstairs to my room. When he got there, he busted the door open and there she was, just as naked as she was when she came into the world. Her breasts were clearly exposed. She then sat up. At that point, my dad could see everything!

"Get out!" he hollered at us. I was so embarrassed and angry. We then packed up and went to stay at the Holiday Inn. It was a newly built hotel. The room was very nice. We spent the next two days at the Holiday Inn having sex and getting to know one another. I didn't anticipate the hell that was getting ready to knock on our door. You see, back in that day, in the south, a black boy and white girl was not looked upon favorably; and yes, we caught hell from society. Her dad and my father wasn't too happy about us being together either, but we didn't care. We called ourselves being in love. One day, I re-introduced Connie to cocaine, which was the worst mistake of my life. We were both using it. And since she was using it, I felt comfortable with buying more and more drugs. We were more happy together when using drugs than when were when we weren't using drugs.

By the age of 23, I was doing crazy things to get more drugs. We got to the point that we didn't want to eat anything; we just wanted to smoke. She began to sell her body while I looked the other way. She even started to do things that I don't particularly care to mention even to this day. But, at that time, I just didn't care. And then, one day, she became pregnant with my son. I did everything possible to make sure that she didn't use drugs at that point because I wanted my child to come into this world healthy—having all ten fingers and toes and being in his right mind, not deformed. So I did everything that I could think of to make sure that she was drug-free. But, of course, I failed miserably. You just can't be around someone everyday, twenty four hours a day, and make a that person do what is right. I discovered that when I wasn't around she was using drugs. I remember one time, while we were staying with my parents, I was searching under the bed and discovered evidence that she had been using the night before while pregnant with my son, Steven. Talk about being angry! I was angry! When she got home, I called and asked her if she used drugs last night. She lied and said no. I went crazy and hit her. She then ran downstairs and out of the house. I caught up to her on the side of the house and began yelling at her angrily. My mom was looking out of the window at us, and Connie said something rude to her. I can't recall exactly what was said, but whatever it was, all I remember is taking my hat off of my head and my hat going across her face. My mom then knocked on the window and yelled, "Steve, what's wrong with you?!!" That was the first time my mother ever heard me use profanity. Connie ran out of the yard and down the street. By the time I caught up with her, my mom was out in the yard calling us back to the house. We went back to the house. My mother instructed Connie to go back into the house while looking in my direction. "Come here, boy," mom said in a serious tone. With my head down, I went over to her. "Look at me," she said. "Do you love me?"

"Yeah ma'am, you know I do."

"Do you love her?"

"Yes ma'am."

"Well, if you love her like you say you do, you wouldn't be hitting on her. How can you look down in her face when you are making love to her and her face is all bruised up from you hitting her and beating on her like that? That's not love, boy! Have you ever seen your father hit me?"

"No ma'am."

"Have you ever seen us fight?"

"No ma'am."

"Well, where you get that from?"

"But momma, she's smoking dope and I don't want my son born deformed," I responded. It didn't dawn on me that maybe she was still smoking dope because I was still smoking dope. I smoked everyday. Since she saw me smoking all of the time and both of us were junkies, it only made sense that she'd want to smoke some dope, too. So, when I wasn't around, of course she was going to smoke—that's what junkies do. From that point on, I stopped hitting her.

Connie and I moved from my parents' house to the Rainbow Forest Apartments in DeKalb County; that's where she had our son, Steven. Thank God that he was born with all of his fingers and toes; he was healthy. I learned that even in the midst of your mess God can still bring about a blessing. It's true that weeping endures only for a night and joy comes in the morning. I stayed with Connie for six years, and during that time I was in and out of jail. I wasn't thinking about what I was doing to myself and Connie. The only thing that mattered to me then was getting drugs so that Connie and I could smoke. I didn't care about anything nor anyone. I remember one night, Connie and I were getting high. We were back in the streets. At this time, we had lost our apartment—and it was cold outside. The wind was blowing and it was raining. There I was with Connie and my son, Steven, dragging them down the street. By this time things had gotten so bad at home that my father didn't want me around his house anytime after 12am. But it was cold. I went to my father's house and knocked on his window. "Who is it?" he asked.

"It's me," I said.

"Me, who?" he asked.

"Stephen."

"What you want?"

"To come in," I replied.

"What time is it?"

"I don't know." Silence. Knock. Knock. Knock.

"Who is it?" Dad asked again.

"It's me."

"Me, who?"

"Stephen."

"What you want?" He asked.

"I want to come in."

"What time is it?"

"I don't know daddy. What . . . Can I come in?"

"What time is it?" He replied.

"I don't know." At that point, I heard my mom enter into my father's room.

"Bishop, you gonna let him in? He got that child outside and it's cold and raining out there," she reminded him.

CHAPTER 3: THE WIFE THAT NEVER WAS

"Go back to bed, woman," dad told her. I never heard another word again from momma that night.

"Daddy! Daddy! Daddy!" I called out.

"What?" dad asked.

"Can I come in?"

"What time is it?" he asked yet a third time. Frustrated, I left and went across the street to an old abandoned house. The floor was wet and muddy; there were dirty, muddy rags; blankets were lying everywhere; rats were all over the place and an old broken down couch was sitting next to the wall. I got my wife and my son and we laid on that couch. I felt around and found a muddy blanket. I searched for the least muddiest blanket I could find. Talk about pig pin? Talk about waddling in the mud? I not only covered myself under a dirty blanket, but I covered my son—my baby boy who I prayed to God for, the one I loved so much—and the woman that brought my son into the world under that muddy blanket. Because of my actions and decisions I had the both of them in that muddy, abandoned house and under a dirty, filthy, muddy, nasty, stinking blanket. I was dragging them to hell with me.

You have to be cautious of the company you keep because your company can drag you down if you're not careful. I was bad company for my wife and my son. I was bad company even for myself. The crazy thing is I was blaming everyone else for my situation. I was blaming my father, I was blaming my brothers, my sisters, my friends; I was blaming everyone except for myself. I was too selfish to take the responsibility for my own actions. Me, Connie, and our son made it through the night; but the next morning, instead of going out to find something to eat, I went looking for another hit of dope. While I was gone, Connie took our son back across the street to my parents' house. When I got back to that old abandoned house, Connie was there all by herself. I asked her where Steve was. She told me he was across the street at my parents' house. I was like 'Okay. Cool. Now I don't have to worry about him.' She and I went out and started doing all type of things: she began selling her body while I looked the other way. I started breaking into houses to steal. Connie and I soon figured that breaking and entering was the best move—we found that we could get a lot of stuff, which also meant more coke, that way. Eventually, that became my profession: being a burglar. I would break into people's houses all times of day. It didn't matter what time it was. I considered myself a professional; that is, until I started getting caught. I would get caught and then get sent to jail. While I was in jail, Connie was out in the streets smoking. I would worry about her while locked up, hoping that no one would attempt to take her away from me. I would do a little time and then get out and go right back to smoking dope.

I remember once when Connie and I were staying off Glenwood. I came home after doing 90 days at Rockdale Stone Mountain Probation Boot Camp. When I knocked on the front door, another woman opened it. She asked me who I was. I told her my name. I then asked the woman if Connie staying there. She told me to wait a minute, and then she shut the door. When my Connie came to the door, she had on a robe; and under the robe, she was butt naked. My best friend (or my so-called friend) was there. Evidently, my so-called best friend was tapping my girl. Now imagine that. I put both of them out. Connie went crazy because her friend did not have a place to stay. While she was fussing, I thought to myself, "Why did you put her out? That's another girl." I had thought of a plan to bring her back. So, after I got settled in, I went out and found Connie's friend.

Every morning, I would get up at 4 am to use the bathroom. (When I was in prison, we were conditioned to get up at 4 am.) Connie's friend slept in the living room on the couch. But this one particular morning, on my way back to the bedroom from the bathroom, Connie's friend turned her head to face me, and when our eyes met, nothing else needed to be said. We went into the bedroom and had sex while Connie was sleeping in the next room. She and I had sex for around two to three more times, which led to me contracting a disease. I then called my parents' house and told my momma. She told me that my father would be over to take me to the hospital.

When my dad arrived to pick me up, he was laughing. Perhaps, this is because he didn't like Connie in the first place. When I got home from the hospital with my medicine, I tried to hide it but Connie found it; at that point, I told her everything that happened. "Yes, I had sex with your friend in the living, on the patio, upstairs over at Pete's house, and downstairs in the abandoned apartment, and that's how I caught this disease," I told her.

"I'm gonna kill her!" Connie screamed.

"I figured to myself that, hell, if I'm gone, there's nothing I can do about what you do. I can't miss what I can't measure. That was always told to me, so I didn't think you cared," I then said.

After my best friend left, things went back to normal (if you want to call smoking dope normal). I found myself falling deeper and deeper into my addiction. My son, which was two at the time, was with Connie and me, and every time we smoked I would put him in the back room. As a result of this, our son was being neglected. My apartment became the hit house in the neighborhood. All of the junkies, dope smokers, crackheads (whatever you want to call them) came to my house to smoke. I thought I was being smarter than everyone else because I would charge $10 and a dime to come into my house to hit their dope. They would smoke and smoke and smoke, and at the end of the night, I would sell the same dope they gave me back to them.

We started getting noticed by the property manager and I began noticing the police standing across the street looking up at my unit. I thought I was careful. That's why people call crack a mind altering drug: it changes your whole perception of life; it changes your view of everything; what you think is up is actually down, what you consider down is actually sideways, and what is sideways is actually straight; everything you see is the opposite of what it really is. I did not want to go back to jail, but I did nothing to stop myself from going back. As a matter of fact, I speeded up the process of going back to jail. I remember going home one day—this was the last time Connie and I were together. By this time, Connie and I had gotten married. We were married for 45 days before I got locked up for burglary. On this particular day, when I came home, there was another man lying in my bed butt naked. I finally discovered then what is meant by "tunnel vision" and "a crime of passion." I looked at that man lying in the bed, then at my wife, then at that man again, and then I hit my wife. That was the last time I ever hit her. After striking her, I went straight into the kitchen, grabbed a knife, then ran back into the bedroom with the intention of sticking that knife right in that man's chest and killing him. The only thing that stopped me was my brother's voice. He was yelling my name at the top of his voice—"Steve!!" When I heard my name being yelled, I snapped back to the present moment, then I dropped the knife, balled my hand up, and went right across that man's face with a right cross. I knocked him out of the bed. While he was naked we were fighting. He then fell on my son. I then pulled him off of my son and went crazy on him. After the fight, I looked at the guy and asked him if she had ever mentioned to him that I was coming home. He said yes.

"Well, didn't she tell you that I would snap?" I asked.

"Yes," he replied.

"Well, why did you stay? Oh you must have thought that you could beat me?" I asked. "It's okay, though. You can have her." I then turned to my wife and told her to get my son, his paperwork, his clothes, and everything else that belongs to him and give it to me. She hurried into the other room and got everything that belonged to our son. I took him and I then left. Strangely, I kept going back to her because I thought I loved her.

One day, the strangest thing happened to me. I know I had to do this for me. I loved my wife, Connie, but I needed to know how she felt about me. So, one day, I went back over to her house. We sat down in the living room and talked. She told me how much she loved the other guy I found in our bedroom. She explained that even while she was with me for six years, he was always on her mind. He was her first love and she always wanted to get back with him. While hearing those words my heart was being ripped apart; but strangely, it was being mended back together at the same time. During that process, my heart was growing hard—very hard. You could say a hatred was forming in my heart towards her. We would still get together, smoke, and have sex, but we were doing it behind his back because she was now his girl, not mine. She would come over to my neighborhood and I would put her out in the streets to go sell her body and make some money for me. She was only a whore to me now. "B****, go get my money so we can smoke!" I would tell her. And she obeyed gladly. I was a terrible man, a troubled man. I was hurting and scared. Some days, I would cry out to God, but I figured He didn't hear me.

I remember walking down the street one morning at 2 am—by then, I had accepted the fact that I was a junkie and had come to believe that was how I was going to die. So I decided that I was going to go out in style. I thought to myself if I was going to be a junkie, then I was going to be the best junkie that I could be. I started burglarizing houses, not even caring whose house it was or whether or not the residents were even home. One day, I broke into a house to burglarize it but heard a noise that scared me. I then ran out the house and down the street. But I thought to myself I needed to go back because I needed to get the money because I had someone waiting for me, ready to give me $100 if I got them a microwave.

So I went back to the house and around to the back door, which was still open. I went in through the back door and headed for the microwave in sight. I couldn't see, so I began searching for the light switch. When I clicked the light switch on, I heard a noise behind me. I then turned around only to see a man looking at me with rage in his eyes and a large shotgun in his hands. He hollered, "I'm going to kill you, you M***** F*****!!" The only thing that went through my mind was "Run!!!" So, I ran past him, out the door, and around the house. I then heard a loud "BOOM!!!" behind me.

"Oh my God, he's trying to kill me!" I shouted. So, I started running even faster. "BOOM!!!" I heard it again. Have you ever seen one of this movies where a person is running but then they fall while the monster or killer is right behind them, and the only thing you can think at that time is 'Why are they falling?', especially when there is nothing there that would cause them to fall? I finally found out why they'd fall. I fell for no reason at all. I said to myself, "Why you falling?! Get up!" I finally got up, and was running faster than I'd ever ran. I finally hid behind a tree that was in his yard. I then looked across the street and said to myself, "If I make it across street and beside that house I might be able to get away." I then took off running. I was running for my life . . . literally. I then heard it again: "BOOM!!!" But this time, when the man shot at me, he connected. It felt like a group of bumblebees stung me in my back. I managed to get up off of the ground, then catapulted myself over a fence and landed on my stomach. When I landed, I said, "Oh man, he got me!" I crawled under some bushes and I started to pray: "Please God, don't let him come and shoot me again. Please God, don't let him come shoot me again."

It's funny how when we get in trouble we always call on God. When I was breaking into that man's house, trying to take his belongings, I wasn't thinking about God then; but now that I'm about to lose my life, I began to think about God. I knew God exists.

I laid on the ground for what seemed like an eternity, although it was only a few minutes. I then got up and hopped over to the next street where I collapsed. A couple of people that I knew came over to me and asked me what happened. I told them I got shot. They asked me who shot me. I said I didn't know—that I was robbed. Imagine that!

One guy I knew named Charles pulled my shirt up, looked at my back, and then said, "Oh man, they messed you up." I was thinking I needed to get out of there because, believe it or not, I was concerned with getting some more dope to smoke. By this time, everyone in the neighborhood who was awake at that time came out to see what all of the commotion was about. There I was, laying on the ground, shot. Someone said, "Call the police!" Another person said they called the paramedics, and someone else said they were calling my family.

I thought to myself, "The paramedics: I can do. My family: I can do. The police: I can't do. You can call anyone but the police." I knew that should the police come, I was going back to jail, and that wasn't the time for me to go back to jail. Still, someone called the police, paramedics, and my family. When I looked up, my sister and my niece was standing over me. The police finally arrived. An officer asked me what happened. Of course,

CHAPTER 3: THE WIFE THAT NEVER WAS

I lied: "I got shot," I replied.

"By who?" the officer asked.

"I don't know. Man, they pulled up on me and said, 'Give me your money!' I told them I didn't have no money. They pulled out a gun and I started running, and they shot me," I said.

"What color was the car?" the officer asked.

"Blue."

"What else?"

"I don't know, man! Just get me to the hospital!" I responded.

I was taken to the hospital. That night, the police got a phone call from the victim. The officer then came to the hospital where I was to confront me. He said, "Yeah, Mr. Howard, Mr. Crouch called and said he had to shoot somebody that was in his house." The officer then asked me if I had anything to say. I just looked at him and said, "Naw, man. You got me." I was later taken to jail. I went straight from the hospital to the county jail. I stayed in the county jail for around 45 days; after that, I went home and went right back to the drugs. I didn't care that I just got shot, was in a wheelchair, I taken to jail, I was blessed to be walking around again. I didn't care that I could have died or been paralyzed. None of that was on my mind. What was on my mind was getting high.

CHAPTER 4:
FOR THE G'S
AND THE HUSTLAS

I WAS OUT IN THE STREETS SMOKING MY BACK OUT again. My habit got so bad that I would break in multiple houses in a single day. I had this little song that I would sing every time I left out of a house—it was a song by Snoop Dogg entitled "G'z and Hustlas": "This is for the g'z and this is for the hustlas, to the hustlas now back to the g'z."

The devil has a way of doing things. He has a way of exposing you to things you shouldn't be exposed to. Demons will guide you whenever you are doing their will. It amazes me even today that whenever I would break into someone's house—a house I had never been in before—I would almost intuitively go straight to where the safe was, where the money was, where their stash was every time. It's like I was being guided by spirits. Just like God can guide us by His Spirit, Satan can also guide you; and that's why you have to be careful and prayed up: Satan is very cunning and powerful. But I praise God that

He will spoil ours and the enemy's plans. We serve a God that will step in and block everything that the enemy is trying to do in our lives. God is full of grace and mercy. God will see you through regardless of what the enemy is trying to do. Even when you don't know what's going on in your life, best believe that God is there and He has a plan for you; He knows what is best for you. I thank God that He saw me through this part of my life, that He didn't let me get killed in the streets and die in my sins. Someone was certainly praying for me and covering me while I was out of my mind.

I should have died in those streets several times. One time, I recall overdosing on drugs. I had a little money on me, so I called the dope man. He came over and brought me a fifty cent piece of dope (that's about $50 worth of crack). I cut off a piece and put on the straight shooter. When I hit the dope, I began to cough. I never did this before. I hit it again, and I coughed again—for some reason, I coughed every time I smoked this particular dope. When I was done smoking, I went outside. It was cold outside. When I got to the bottom of the stairs, I started to regurgitate. All I remember was something white coming out of my mouth and then hitting the ground hard. The girl that was with me started hollering my name over and over: "Steve! Steve! Steve! Get up!" She then began to cry for help: "Help! Help! Somebody help me!" But no one came. I was lying on the ground in a puddle of freezing cold water. When I regained consciousness, I crawled over to the apartment wall, leaned up against it, and then tried to stand up, but I was too weak to stand. I then told the girl to go and get Calvin, my godfather who I was staying with at the time. She went and got Calvin. He arrived and helped me back to his house instead of taking me to the hospital. I took my clothes off, wrapped myself up in a blanket, and then laid on the floor, shivering all night. I could have died that day. I should have died that day. The next day, I called my supplier and told him what happened. He then told me that several of his other clients had the same thing happen to them and that one of them ended up in the hospital. He explained to me that it was the pot that he used to cook his dope in: instead of cleaning the pot, he just used it as is. The chemicals that were in the pot were cooked into the dope. That's what made everyone sick. I thank God for intervening and stopping the plans of the enemy (Satan) that day...like He had done so many times before. But that was my second near death experience as a result of smoking crack. Unfortunately, there were more experiences to come. God is not only good to us, but He is patient with us.

Living with Calvin was a roller coaster ride. As I mentioned before, Calvin spoiled me when I was a child. But now, I wasn't a child; I was a grown man. Even still, I was still spoiled and selfish like a piece of meat that's been sitting in a refrigerator way too long. I lied to Calvin everyday just to get money. When a junkie wants to get money, they will think of some super duper lies. I don't know where those lies came from. My mother always told me, "Boy, you can look me in my eyes and tell a bold face lie!" And I could. I would use this ugly skill against people to get what I wanted; and sadly, I used it extensively on Calvin because he was always good to me, he always came to my rescue no matter how much I messed up, and he always put up with me and gave me everything that I wanted.

One day, Calvin got up to go to work; and after he left for work, I went next door and burglarized his neighbor's apartment. The next day, after Calvin went to work, I burglarized another one of his neighbor's homes; however, this time the police had a good lead as to who it was and where to look. One day, while I was at work, I noticed a police officer talking to my supervisor. The two then looked over my way. My supervision then motioned to me to come to them. At first, I thought about running, but I knew better; so I went over to them instead. When I approached them, the officer asked me if I was Stephen Howard. I said yes. Immediately, the officer arrested me and took me to jail. When I got to the jail I was taken to an interrogation room. An officer came and sat down in front of me and presented me with a picture of Calvin. I asked him why he had Calvin's picture, to which he replied that they had to lock him up as well. I said, "Please let him go. He had no idea that I broke into that house. He has no clue."

"Yes. I'm glad you admitted to this because he looked a little timid back there," the officer said. They then released Calvin and locked me up. Yeah, I was mad, but Calvin was even more pissed off with me. When I got out of jail and went back to Calvin's house, he immediately confronted me and said,

"Gotta go! Get out!"

Today, I don't blame him. I understand why he kicked me out. But back then, I actually thought he was wrong. 'You just don't throw nobody out like that, especially when he's just got out of prison' I thought to myself. My mind was WHOOPED! I thought Calvin just didn't understand me, so I left his house with a heart full of hatred and contempt; but my hatred wasn't necessarily directed towards him, but it was directed at the whole world. I felt like the world owed me something and that I was determined to collect however I could.

I moved back home and started burglarizing homes left and right. My need for crack grew out of control. At first, I would break into houses around my home: I would go to the house next door, the one down the street, the one around the corner. I was lost in my mind, asleep to the damage that I was causing not only to myself but to my family, never thinking about the fact that I was heading for a prison cell. Crack became my food. I'd wake up, smoke, and often pass out on crack. I remember breaking into one house in the hood, and afterwards, the owner's sons came looking for me. It's really bad when everyone in the neighborhood knows who the neighborhood theft is. When that home owner's sons found me, I was high as a kite. One of the boys asked me for their belongings, and, of course, I did not have them; and before I knew what happened, "BOOM!!!" right across my face. Man, I saw stars, the moon, the sun, and every other planet in the solar system! After that, all of the boys began to beat and stomp on me like I was a dog. But you don't even treat a dog in this way. There I was on the ground, balled up in the fetal position, attempting to protect myself. I had no fight in me. In my feeble mind, I believed I deserved and even needed that beat down. It would be payment for the wrongs that I had done. After those boys finished beating on me, I got up and went home to lick my wound and figure out how I could get some more crack.

After I healed up enough, I was back at it again. One particular day, I met a lady that stayed in our hood. Her husband was a good man, but she, like me, smoked crack. So we hit it off. You know what they say: Birds of a feather flock together. We would smoke together. One day, we had no money; she then told me about some money she had at home, which she hid…in a Bible. Oh God, I'm going to hell, I thought.

She told me to go to her house to get the money. She said I would see the Bible, and all I had to do was open it to a certain page and the money would be there. I did it. I got the money and then hurried off to go get more dope. It was off to the race again. We were smoking again, and once we ran out, we would come out of our cave, put our heads together, and figure out a way to get some more dope. After I would get some money, we would smoked it all up. One day, her son stepped to me and accused me of stealing their money. I did not deny taking it, but I tried to explain what happen. But before I knew it, "BOOM!" right across my head. There I was again, back on the ground trying to protect myself. When her son got tired of beating on me I was so relieved. I began to get up, still trying to explain to him that his momma told me where that money was and even instructed me to go and get it. At that point, he became angry with his mother for not intervening with the truth and preventing us from fighting—that is, if you count my face cowering while his fist connects to it a fight. (I wouldn't recommend this very, very dangerous form of fighting.) He then felt bad for what he did to me, and I once again felt that I deserved everything that I had coming to me.

CHAPTER 4: FOR THE G'S AND THE HUSTLAS

There were times when just before smoking a piece of crack, I would actually look at that piece of crack and have a conversation with it. I would say to it, "I hate you. You got control over my life!" I would say to it, "I hate you! This is not what I'm supposed to be doing, and I wish you would let me go! Leave me alone! Leave Me Alone!!!!! You don't give a **** whose life you destroy, do you?! You ain't nothing but the devil and I hate the day you came into my life!!" And after delivering this heart wrenching speech to the piece of crack, I would put that piece of white death on a glass tube, put it up to my mouth, place my lighter under it, and began to inhale it while shedding tears.

Have you ever done something wrong and, at first, you felt bad about it, but as you contented to do it, you felt less convicted and it got easier to do it? That means your heart is becoming calloused. After a while, you'll no longer give a rats butt about what you are doing. After a while, you'll just give up resisting the urge to do what you know is wrong. The Bible calls this having a "reprobate mind" in Romans chapter 1. That was the state of mind I was in. I JUST DIDN'T CARE!!!! Breaking into people's houses, smoking, and drinking were things I was caught up in. And what's even worse is, as things became very routine, I began to feel the need for something more. It began to be boring, no fun just breaking into people's homes, so I had to find a way to make my crimes worthwhile. I started breaking into 3 to 4 houses a day. But even that became a boring routine, so I started venturing out into other neighborhoods. "Man," I thought to myself, "I hit the jackpot! These people are so gullible. They don't even lock their car doors or the doors to their homes." That made them ease targets to me. But a trap was being set for me by the enemy without me realizing it.

CHAPTER 5:
WILL REHAB WORK?

WHEN YOU ASK GOD FOR SOMETHING, HE hears you. I had prayed for divine intervention, and it came. I wasn't, however, prepared for the method in which God would intervene in my life in an attempt to pull me off of the destructive path I was on. He works in unusual ways.

I was back in my old neighborhood staying with my parents again; and as usual, I had a burning desire to smoke some crack. I remember waking up one morning and deciding that I needed to get out and find some money for dope; but this time, instead of going to the other neighborhoods that were easy targets for me, I decide to do just one hit (or lick) at home. I went around the corner and I broke into a house, not knowing that my neighbor was driving by, and she noticed me going through the window. I went inside of the house and took what I could use to make a quick buck with, sold that merchandise, took the money and got high. After that I broke into more houses and I got high some more. I decided to stay around the neighborhood and break into houses since it was quicker and I was closer to home.

One night in January of 1995, I broke into a house, stole some merchandise, sold it, got some dope, and then went to a friend of mine's house to smoke it. My friend was a girl that I liked. I wanted to spend time with her, but she was much older than me and never indicated that she was interested in me. But one day, she apparently noticed that I really liked being around her. I would always go over to her house so that we could get high together. Eventually, she decided that she would be my girlfriend. I felt like I was living on top of the world! I had an older woman that was my girl. One night, we were rolling around in the bed when I received a phone call from my mom who told me that one Detective Favor wanted to see me. I inquired more about who Detective Favor was and what he wanted. My mom then told me that he claimed he only needed to talk to me and that he wasn't going to lock me up. So I told her I would be at her house the next morning and would give him a call then. Around this time, my son was three years old. The next morning, when I arrived at my parent's home, my son was in the living room sitting on the floor playing with his Power Ranger action figures. I picked up the phone and called Detective Favor. He simply said that he needed to talk to me. Nothing more. I said okay and told him that I would be there at my parent's house—that I wasn't going anywhere. After that, I dozed off and fell asleep on the couch. I was later awakened by a knock on the door. It was Detective Favor along with another detective. I opened the door and they entered into the house. "Are you Steven Howard?" Detective Favor asked.

"Yes," I replied.

CHAPTER 5: WILL REHAB WORK?

"Steven, I want to warn you that you have the right to remain silent. Anything you say will be held against you in a court of law."

"Wait! Wait! Wait! What's going on? You said you wasn't going to lock me up! You said you need to talk to me," I interrupted while they were placing handcuffs on me.

"Yes, but we need to talk at the precinct," he replied.

"Awe, man!"

My son was looking at me, wondering why those men were taking his daddy away. He began to ask, "Why you taking my daddy?" I than asked Detective Favor if he would please let me speak with my son for a minute. He allowed me to. I leaned down and said to my son,

"Son, it's going to be okay. I'll be home soon, okay. Don't worry. Daddy will be home soon."

The detectives then took me outside, put me in their car, and then drove me around the neighborhood to let me see the houses I had broken into. When they drove pass by one house, I turned my head and looked the other way as if I didn't know what they were doing. One detective looked back at me in the rear view mirror and then he said to the other detective, "Yeah, he knows. Look at him. He knows he broke into that house."

"Man, just get me downtown so we can get this over with, okay!" I said.

"Okay," one of the detectives replied.

The detectives took me downtown and booked me. I sat in jail for about a week before I saw a public defender. When the public defender came, I could have sworn that she was working for the prosecutor. She explained to me the charges I was charged with and that what the prosecutor really wanted was to send me to jail. But I didn't like how my public defender was talking.

"Mr. Steven Howard, you know you did these burglaries and you need to take the time they are offering you, which was two years," my public defender said.

"I'm not trying to take no two years! I got a son at home! I need to get back on the street!" I was really thinking I didn't want to take the two years because I wanted to get back to smoking drugs. "I'm not trying to take no two years! I want to go home!!" I said to the public defender. She then left. I was angry. "You supposed to be my lawyer!" I said to myself. "And you trying to send me to prison! Man get out of my face!"

I went back to my cell, angry. About a week later, my lawyer returned and said, "Mr. Howard, they got you good. The witness says she recognize you from the back of your head, and I see you have another charge where you got shot."

"Yes," I said.

"Well, he said that you broke into his house and he shot you," she explained.

"But he shot me in my back and that's in Atlanta. This is Dekalb County. What do that have to do with this? I was going through his yard and he came out as I'm walking through and said 'I'm going to kill you, M*****F*****!' and just went crazy and shot me in my back. So, how is it that that case and this case is going to convict me?"

I knew that I had them because both witnesses said they recognized me only from the back: one shot me in the back and the other said that she recognized me only from the back of my head. I was thinking to myself, "You don't have me. I'm going to get off scotch-free. And I will be able to do what I want to do again: break into more houses, smoke more dope, drink more liquor, get more girls, do what I want to do. I got you beat." I felt confident that I had the case beat. But suddenly, while I was sitting on my bunk one day, I heard a voice. The strange voice said, "You asked me for help?"

"Yeah," I responded.

"Well, now is the time that you can receive it. Go ask for help," the voice instructed me. I immediately jumped up ran to the phone and called my mom. She answered the phone.

"Mom, I need help. They trying to give me two years in prison, but if I do two years I'm going to get out and start back smoking dope. So, this ain't gonna do me no good. Can I please get some help? Can they send me to a rehab or some place where I can get some help? I'm tired. I'm tired of coming to jail. I'm tired of living like this. I need help."

"Well, what do you want me to do?" my mom asked. I asked her to call the District Attorney and tell them that I was on drugs and was an addict and that I needed help, not imprisonment. "Okay, call me back later," mom said before getting off of the phone.

I hung up the phone with the hope in my spirit that I will finally be free from crack cocaine. I called my mother back. She said to me that the DA wanted her to come to court on that Monday. Oh, man! I was filled with high expectations then. I knew help was around the corner. I just knew I would finally be free from this beast, I would be free from this demon, I would be free to do the things that I used to when in my right mind and live the life that I used to live; that I would finally be free to be me again. Prior to that Monday (the day of my scheduled appearance in court), I was walking around the jail in a daze; my spirit was filled with so much hope.

Monday rolled around and my name was called that morning to go to court. As I stood before the judge, my lawyer was there along with the DA; my mother and father were there as well. It was my time to stand before the judge. The DA stood up on my behalf as my lawyer. The DA said to the judge, "Judge, Mr. Steven Howard's family is here. His mother called me and said that he is asking for help. He is on drugs and they don't know what to do. She said they took him to a rehab and the rehab told him to come back after being 24 hours of being clean; so they never could receive help for their son. They are asking the court to please send him to some kind of program that will help him leave drugs alone."

The judge looked at my public defender (I call her my public "pretender") and she was looking all confused, not knowing what to say or how to react; so, she simply said, "Okay Judge, whatever they say I'm with it." The Judge asked,

"Well, where is his mother?"

"She's over there," the DA said, pointing at my mom. The judge asked my mother if she wanted to say anything. My mother then stepped up before the judge and pretty much repeated every word the DA said. Then the judge looked over at my father and asked him if he had anything to say. My father then stepped up to the judge and basically repeated everything my mother said. Then the judge looked over at me and then said,

CHAPTER 5: WILL REHAB WORK?

"Your parents truly love you."

"Yes sir," I responded.

While this was going on, I was thinking to myself, "This might work. I am going to finally be free from this living nightmare. The gates of hell will finally be closed and I'll be able to live a normal life again." The judge then asked the DA,

"What about New Start? Do we have any beds open over there?"

"We have to check on it, your honor. It's a 9 month program, but he can stay in jail until a bed becomes open," the DA replied.

"OK," the judge said to the DA. He then looked at me and said, "Mr. Howard, you are getting another chance. I am giving you five years probation and nine months in the New Start Rehabilitation Treatment Program. However, if you do not complete this program and if you come back before me, you will have eight years to do in prison. Do you understand me?"

"Yes sir," I responded enthusiastically. The judge then turned to my mother and said,

"Mrs. Howard, we are going to do everything that we possibly can to help him become clean. It is good that he is asking for help; however, he got to put in the work. This is not going to be easy, and it's up to him."

"I understand. We just want our son back. He's a good boy. He just got caught up with drugs. Thank you so much, your honor," my mom replied. I went back to jail and waited for a bed to become available. About two months later one became available and I was sent to the rehab.

Chapter 6:
WORST FEAR REALIZED

WHILE IN THE NEW START REHABILITATION Program, it was difficult at first not living life on my terms. I had to face feelings and emotions that I was so used to suppressing. But as time progressed, the process became easier. I began working the program. I had worked my way up the ranks so that I found myself moving to the next phase in the program. I was serious about my recovery. Everything was going smoothly...until three months later, when I had reached the 3rd phase of the program—in this phase you are allowed to go outside of the facility to work. One day, I was returning from work when all of a sudden some of the guys that were out at the store gave me the heads up. They told me everything that had transpired while I was at work. When I got off of the bus and returned to the center, one guy said, "Man, Howard, they done kicked your butt out!"

"What!?!?" I said.

"Yeah, man. They said you invited somebody to your 'Johnson.'"

"What?! Who?! When!?" I asked in disbelief.

"Man, I'm not saying; I'm just giving you the heads up," the man responded.

"OK," I said, walking fast now to the center. I just knew good and well that the program's facilitators weren't going to believe a lie that had been put out on me; however, things were a little different than I thought when I got in the door. Everyone was looking at me, shaking their heads, saying, "I'm sorry." All of the girls were crying as if someone had died. I realized then that everyone believed the lie and that I was gone.

"Man, I got to report to the probation officer now and let her know what happened," I thought. "Oh boy, what's the judge gonna say?" The judge had already said to me that if I ever stood before him again I was going to prison. I had this girl I called myself going with at the time. I was about to lose her also because of this bold face lie. But I had to keep my cool. I had to let everyone know that I was still going to stay clean. "I don't need y'all," I said to myself, lying. Telling the truth was frightening. I called my girlfriend told her what just happened and asked her to come and pick me up. She did. I went to stay with her. Things were going great for about a week, then we had to move because her supervisor informed us that we couldn't stay in a personal care home. But her supervision then told us she had a rooming house in Decatur and a house on River Road we could live.

My girlfriend and I moved into one of those rooming houses, which was really just a small upstair room. This room was so small you had to bend over to stand; you could barely walk in there. The girl I was going with started acting crazy on me, so I decided to get crazy too—I decided to cheat on her with her friend. I felt like a fool afterwards. But the damage was done. I never told her about the affair. We ended up moving again to River Road into an eight bedroom home that sat on 10 acres of land. The landlord gave me a car. The only thing I had to do with it was get the keys. I wasn't doing drugs then and I was determined not to use that stuff. I was working every day, making good money, and I had a fine girl staying with me in a big, nice house. What else could a man ask for? Why would I want to mess all of that up?

Things began to unravel when one day I came home to find that my girlfriend wasn't there. I waited and waited, but she never came home. (Oh, did I tell you that she was an ex junkie, too?) I started to worry if something happened to her. It was about seven in the evening and this wasn't consistent with her everyday routine. I called around and no one heard from her. My sponsor called me and I told him what was going on, and all he said to me was, "Well, don't use drugs."

"Yeah, I know," I said. About an hour later he came by the house.

"Get in the car," he said. I did. "Where do you think she may be?"

"Over in Kirkwood," I responded. So we went to Kirkwood. We rode around the neighborhood looking for her. Finally, we got a lead to her whereabouts; however, I couldn't go in there because I didn't know which house she was held up in. My sponsor took me home and asked me if I was going to be OK. I said yeah. So he left me there.

I was determined that I was not going to use drugs. I called my brother and told him what was going on. I was done with this girl. "Oh, she got me twisted. I don't know who she thinks I am," I said to myself. I was done. I asked my brother for the name of the girl who was over at his house the other day.

"What girl?" he asked.

"You know, the one that was over your house on the 4th of July," I responded.

"Oh, you talking about my wife's friend?" he asked.

"Yeah."

"Hold up," he said. My brother's wife then got on the phone and I asked her about her friend.

"Oh, she's my assistance," his wife responded.

"Ok, where is she?" I asked.

"You like her?"

"Yeah."

"OK, I'll call her. You want her to call you?"

"Yeah."

About ten minutes later I got a call from the girl and we talked on the phone for a good while. We made plans to meet up. I then called my dad and asked him to come and get me. He and my older brother came. I packed up everything that belonged to me and put it in the truck of my dad's car. I left all of my old girlfriend's things behind. The next day, while at work, I got a call from my sister-in-law. After that, I got another call from her assistant who I was trying to hook up with. After that call, I receive a sudden, unexpected call from the crazy woman who used to be my girlfriend. "What you want?" I asked her.

"To talk," she responded.

"About?"

"Us," she said.

"There is no us."

"I need to see you."

"I'm at work. I'll talk to you later," I said before hanging up the phone. About an hour later, I got called up to the front office of my job. When I got to the office, there she was: my ex girlfriend. She decided to come all the way to my job.

"What are you doing here?" I asked her.

"We need to talk."

"OK. Let's talk outside," I said to her, not wanting her in the building. We then went outside.

"How dare you leave me?" she said.

"What?" I said, shocked.

"I come home and you are gone and my clothes and stuff are everywhere!" she responded.

"Oh, you must thought I was like all those other guys you use to date, huh! Look, I ain't got time for this. Wherever you were the other night, you can go back there. I'm done."

"Well I…I think I'm just gonna kill myself," she said.

"Well, die then, m*****f*****!" I responded.

"You wasn't all that anyway," she said.

"You was just convenience for me," I responded.

"How dare you! I hate you! I hate you!" she then yelled. That was the last time I talked to or heard anything from her again. I started talking to my sister-in-law's assistant. By week number two, I had moved in with her. Things were going fine, but there was still something missing.

I went to work every day, but soon, I started back

drinking. My intake became more and more as the weeks went by. The next thing I knew, I was back in my old neighborhood drinking. One day, I was in the hood at a woman's house that I used to like when I was younger. I was sitting on her front porch waiting for her to come home when another friend of hers came over. Both of us were sitting on the porch waiting for her to come home. When she finally came home, she said, "Hey, y'all. What y'all doing here?"

"It's been a long time since I've seen you. I just came to see you," I said. To make a long story short, she sent the other guy home; and when she looked at me, she had already made up in her mind that I was going to be hers that night. Talk about dream come true! My wildest dream came true that night; however, this dream quickly turned into a nightmare. I found myself going over to her house everyday. One thing led to another and I was back off to the races again smoking crack. I started to disregard my family as well as my responsibility to this woman who had nothing good going on for herself except for sex. One day, I was given an ultimatum by the woman I was living with. Now mind you: she didn't know that I was back out there on drugs; she just assumed that I was a drunk. She was tired of me coming home late. I wasn't there for the boys anymore, and I didn't want to go to the movies or on date nights any more. I became withdrawn from her as well as life in general.

I was given an ultimatum: "Steve, you got to make a decision: it's gonna be the beer or me," she said. Oh man, that was all I needed to get out of that relationship. Now, I had a reason to escape. I asked myself, "Who do she think she is? Oh no, you didn't just give me an ultimatum. I'll show you that you don't run nothing. The nerve of you!" All the while, I was really rejoicing because felt that I had a legitimate reason to leave her, to cut ties with my responsibilities to her; that I was now free again to smoke as much dope as I wanted without having to answer to anyone. So I quickly packed my things and vam-moosed up out of there. I went back to the hood where there was much smoking to be done. I had a lot of catching up to do—that was my thinking. I ran to the other woman's house and explained to her my situation, and she responded just as I expected: "Oh, this is your home because you are my man. I was wondering how long it was going to take to get you here! Now come on, baby. Let momma show you your home."

She took me by my hand and gave me the grand tour of her home. I felt like a king! That night we rolled around in the bed all night having sex. The next morning, when it dawned on me that this was where I was going to be, I decided to go and get some money. I quit my job the next morning—I just didn't show up for work or even call in and provide an explanation for my absence. I simply didn't care anymore. So, I chose instead to go out and rob just to get money for more drugs. I thought I had grown smarter by then. I decided that I wasn't going to break into anymore homes in the neighborhood; but instead, I would find homes in other neighborhoods to burglarize.

It is a well known fact that God is able to reveal the secrets of our hearts as well as the future—in the church we call this prophesying. But I also learned that the devil can show us things as well. I had this strange ability to see houses in vision and see the valuables that were in those houses—to see where those valuables were located and how to get them. Even the meanest dog was not able to stop me from getting what I wanted. I needed a hit and refused to be stopped!

When I'd get a vision of a house to rob in my mind, I would say to everyone present, "I'll be back" like Arnold Schwartznegger, then head out to rob that house. I'd get to the house, and in less than 5 minutes I'd be in and out and heading back home with enough money and merchandise to get high all night and all day the next day. When I got home, everyone would be jumping around like it was Christmas. The crazy thing about dope is if you have money or drugs, you can get anyone who is on dope to do just about anything.

This went on for that whole summer of 1996 until the day that I had to go to court. I knew where I was going: to prison. As that day approached, my fear and anxiety grew. And finally, when I stood before the judge, my worse fear was realized. My probation officer was there. I knew that there wasn't a good report coming from that direction. Court began and my name was called. My case was brought before the judge: "Yes, your honor. Stephen was order to complete the New Start Drug Rehabilitation Program and he did not complete it. He was thrown out for inviting someone to his personal private part. He was working for a while until he was fired. He failed the drug test given unto him; therefore, judge, I recommend that Stephen complete his time in prison." The judge then looked over to the DA and the DA said,

"Yes, your honor. I agree with his probation officer." The judge then looked over at me and said,

"Mr. Howard, the last time you stood before me

CHAPTER 6: WORST FEAR REALIZED

I warned you that if I see you again, if you stand before me, I was going to send you to prison, son."

"Yes sir."

"Mr. Howard, I'm going to give you 8 years in the Georgia prison system."

Chapter 7:
JUST ANOTHER JAIL

My HEART DROPPED INTO MY STOMACH. My time was up. I knew that it was over. No more dope. No more liquor. No more women. No more…anything. It was all over. I was going to prison for eight years. The officers took me back to the holding cell and then to the county jail. I waited in that jail for about two months until my name was called early on a Tuesday morning: "Steven Howard, pack it up!"

Here we go. I packed up my stuff went down stairs. The officers changed us out and we got us on the bus— handcuffs were on my wrists and chains were on my feet. I felt like an animal being hauled off to the slaughter. The trip to the Jackson State Prison was the longest ride I'd ever taken in my entire life. When we reached the boulevard heading towards the prison, the building came into view; when I saw that big white building and I said to myself "It's just another jail; just another jail; just a bigger jail." I had to psych myself out because I was not going to walk into prison looking like a punk. I had heard so much about prison: how they rape you, how people die in prison, how people are turned out in prison. I was determined to hold myself together. I was determined to go in a man and leave out a man. When the bus pulled up, the officers told us to get off the bus. They took the handcuffs off of us and the chains off of our feet and then told us to line up. We all lined up. Then they told us to follow them, and we marched ourselves into the building.

The room they took us in was cold and it smelled like death. "Take your clothes off," they said. We all took our clothes off. There we were, standing in line; it was about 20 of us. We were butt naked, waiting to be inspected, ready to be degraded, ready to be looked at like a piece of meat, ready to be looked upon and counted as just a number. No longer would my name be Stephen; it would now be EF339296. I became a number in the Georgia prison institution.

After we took our clothes off, the officers told us to look over to our right. We looked over to our right and there was a shower. "Go over there and get in the shower." We took a shower; and while we were in the shower, another inmate prisoner came in and sprayed us down with a lice repellent. After we left the showers, the Sergeant commanded us to go over to the barber's chair. We went to the barber's, sat down in the chair, and he cut all of our hair off. Talk about degrading! I felt so degraded. After that, we were told to get back in line; and once we did, the officers began to run down the "do's and don'ts" in prison: you can't talk after a certain hour; you have to get up at a certain hour; you have to make up your bed; you have to brush your teeth; you have to clean up; and if you don't get up in time to eat, as the saying goes in prison, "Sleep late, lose weight"; you will go out with work detail and work for free, but for the first month you will go through orientation; etc. Orientation was the worst. Orientation was a hell in its own right. You couldn't do anything. But, as time progressed, you learned to adapt to your new environment. I quickly adapted to my environment. I began to walk around with no fear. I knew who I was. I just rolled with the flow. My first prison detail was the kitchen. I hated it. I had to get up every morning around 3 am so that I could be in the kitchen by 4 am so that I could cook for 1800 prisoners.

I found myself getting a little comfortable where I was. Just when I were getting settled, I was placed in B house, and within a month, I was moved again to E house which was next to G house, which was death row. While working in the kitchen, one of my duties was to go to G house. I tell you, the moment the doors would open to G house and you entered through them, you could feel and smell the weight and stench of death; it filled the atmosphere; it was so heavy it would make you want to run for your life.

Not too long after that I asked for a prison detail change because I couldn't deal with the kitchen, I couldn't deal with the people, I couldn't deal with the environment in general. You would go into the freezer and food would be everywhere; you would go out to the warehouse and rats as big as your feet would be running in and out of the food, and you'd have to shake the rat pellets away from the wheat—you had to separate the rat droppings from the bread, and you had to separate the part of the food that the rat did not get to and serve that to the prisoners. I couldn't deal with that anymore. I wanted out. When I put in for a detail change, much to my surprise, I quickly received it. I was put in the barber shop where I had to cut hair. I had a little skill cutting hair, but I wasn't all that. Still, I said, "Yeah, I know how to cut hair. Yes, put me there. Yes, I can do it," not knowing what I was getting myself into.

Now mind you: there is nothing wrong with being a barber if that's your calling, but that wasn't my calling. Every day, I had to get up, go to the barbershop, and cut hundreds of heads. There was one area that was sectioned off for the special needs inmates—it was called F house. In F house, prison doctors would give inmates a certain medicine that would have them walking around like zombies. Some people went to prison pretending to be crazy so that they wouldn't have to work (do prison details); they would be sent to F house as pretenders, but by the time they left F house, they actually were crazy.

I saw many things during my time in prison. When I first arrived in prison, I remember being in the cafeteria. We were in line when a guy entered into the cafeteria, sat on the first row of tables, suddenly fell to the floor, and then died. It took a nurse, a doctor, and a medical team about 5 to 8 minutes to arrive just to see what was going on. I saw boys get beat up and men get raped and turned out—one day, they'd be as hard as nails, and the next day they'd be as soft as cotton. In about three year's time of being at the Jackson State Prison I learned a lot: I learned how to operate backhoes and other heavy equipment; I learned how to construct a fence; I learned how to cut hair; I learned how to cut grass; I learned how to deal with the cold, and I learned how to be alone; I learned how to be lonely, how to cry, how to feel, how to be mad, how to get angry.

CHAPTER 7: JUST ANOTHER JAIL

I met God while in prison. Sadly, when I got out, I left him there. I got out of prison in 1999. Once out, I met a girl and then moved in with her. She was living in Cobb County, Georgia (Cobb County, we call that an acronym for "Come On Back Boy"; that's what C.O.B.B. County stands for).

It wasn't too long before I was back in prison. I stayed out of prison for 45 days before being sent back. I guess I decided to set a record.

I got out of prison and got with this girl. She was nice. She wasn't what I was used to being with, but she would do for the time being. She had a car, an apartment, money, and was willing to spoil me. There I was back out in the streets, back on cocaine (crack). I couldn't keep a job. I was working for the Dekalb County Sanitation Department. I worked there for about a month. About 2 months after losing that job I went and got a job working for Publix. I was at Publix for about a week or two. While working for the Dekalb County as well as Publix, I was burglarizing apartments and houses. Once again, the devil had me in his clutches and he was determined to destroy me. Satan would show me where to go and I would go there; and just as I had seen in the visions Satan gave me, all of the merchandise and money was there. The Bible says in the book of Proverbs that a wicked person will not sleep or rest upon his bed until he have thought of wickedness or until he has come up with a plan to do wickedness to someone. That's the only way that a wicked person is able to sleep. Well, I'm here to inform you that, that was me. I couldn't go to sleep until I thought of a master plan on how to break into someone's house and take everything they had. I would toss and turn all night in the bed until I saw in received a vision of someone's house, money, and merchandise, and then and only then would I turn over and go to sleep.

The next morning I would get up, get dressed like I was going to work, and then I go to the neighborhood I saw in a vision the night before, and break into the house I saw in that vision. I would take the money and merchandise that was there, which I also saw in the vision. After that, I would go home, get all the dope that I could find, go into the bathroom, and smoke. I did this when my girl was at work. She didn't know I was smoking crack in her home because I would hide it so well. Every time I got through with a can, I would crush it and throw it away. I would drive her car and pick her up from work. For a while, I was on point; but soon enough, instead of going to pick her up, I would be at home smoking. After the drugs were gone and I pretty much got myself together I would go and pick her up. I hid my addiction… until one day when I made one of the biggest mistakes of my life. I decided to break into an apartment. When I got there, my eyes stretched bigger than my muscles when they fell on this television. I decided to get that television, which was way too big for me to carry all by myself. At first, I thought I had it, but once I got the television outside I began to struggle. I had a small car that I was trying to put this big, giant television in. It was only me trying to do this. Trying to be smart, I went and knocked on someone's door—as a matter of fact, it was the neighbor of the person whose apartment I just robbed. I went to his house and asked him if he could please help me get the television in the car. This guy knew something was wrong, but he helped me anyway. After we got the television into the car, I thanked him. He then went back into his house and called the police.

I left the apartment and went back to my apartment—we had just moved into a new unit on the third floor. I thought I had it going on. I wanted to fill the apartment with bigger and better stuff. I decided to be smart and get a television. I did not want to steal the television and sell it so that I could go and buy drugs; I wanted the television for my apartment so that I could show my girl that I was there for the long haul and let her know I was able to get beautiful things, too. I wanted to show her that she was not the only one that would bring in nice stuff. What a fool I was! When I got back to my apartment complex, it hadn't dawned on me that I had to go up three flights of stairs; it hadn't dawned on me that I wasn't going to be able to carry that huge television up three flights of stairs all by myself. Once again, since it worked at the last apartment, I figured it would work again at my apartment complex; so I went knocking on doors, seeking help from whoever I could find to help me get the television into my apartment. I knocked on one door and I asked the resident if he could please give me a hand. I told him that I had just purchased that television but was unable to take it to my apartment by myself. He agreed to help me. But when he saw that television, he said, "I cannot pick up that big television. Maybe you can ask maintenance to give you a hand." I happened to observe some Hispanics working on the ground. I went over and asked one of them to give me a hand. I offered to pay him five dollars to help me take that television upstairs to my apartment.

"Five dollars?" the man said.

"Yes, five dollars," I responded. He went and got his friend. "No, no," I said. "I don't have but five dollars. I don't have enough for you and him."

"That's okay. We got it," he said. They grabbed the television and took it up three flights of stairs and into my apartment. Once it was there, I gave them five dollars. At that time, my beeper went off. I looked at the number and it was my girlfriend. She wanted me to come and pick her up. I left the apartment and headed out to go get her. On my way home, I told her,

"Baby, I got a surprise for you!"

"What?" she asked.

"You'll see when we get home." I felt good about myself. But little did I know there was really an ugly surprise waiting for me.

As we pulled up to our apartment complex, I noticed Cobb County had a number of units outside the complex. I asked my girlfriend, "What are they doing here?" It never dawned on me that they were there because of me. We then pulled up, got out of the car, and headed for the stairs. I then asked the officers how they were doing and what was going on. They took one look at me and said,

"You come here." I went to the officer. He then asked, "Where do you stay?"

"Upstairs," I said. He then asked for my ID. I gave it to him. They looked at my ID and then ran a check on it. The darn thing had all of my information on it. It told I had been in prison; it also told them that I was on parole for burglary. I was the culprit they were looking for. Of course, I denied everything saying, "You got the wrong man!"

CHAPTER 7: JUST ANOTHER JAIL

"Oh, we got the right one," one of the officers said. I knew they had me, but it was worth a try. The officers then took me back to the other apartment complex, which I had just robbed. And should it be any shock to you that the same guy that helped me put the television in my car was standing outside talking to the cops? I then claimed that he (the guy that helped me load the television into the car) actually sold me the television in an attempt to place all of the blame on him. I was determined not to go down by myself.

The guy came over to the police car, took one look at me and then said, "Yes, that's him." The cops then closed the door and took me straight to jail. I cried and begged for the officers to let me go, but that was pointless. I was going to jail. Again, I was about to find myself going away for a long time. I would be away from my girl and my son who I'd just lied. See, I promised my son that I was not going anywhere. I made a promise to him that I was there to stay. And now, just look at me: I'm going right back to prison. 'What am I going to do? How is he going to feel now? What is he going to think?' I wondered.

There I was, back in the county jail waiting to go before a judge. I ultimately knew that I was about to go back to prison. About two weeks later, I was back in front of a judge. It was Judge Dorothy Ann Robinson. I will never forget her. When I stood before Ms. Robinson she asked what were the charges against me. The prosecutor told her it was burglary. The judge looked at my paperwork, and, of course, I had burglary upon burglary upon burglary upon burglary on it. It didn't look too good for the home team. She then looked at me and said, "Well, I'm going to give him 20 years to serve 7." My heart dropped to my draws! "Mr. Howard, it seems to me that you will never learn; so, what I'm going to do is do you a favor and I will give you 7 years to complete. I see that you are on drugs and that you try to get help but you keep going through the same cycle; so, maybe after you come out this time, you will be free of your addiction."

"Thank you, your honor," I said. (I didn't mean it, though.)

I went back to my cell and waited to be processed to go to prison. During this time, the girl that I was dating visited me once. She brought my son to see me that one time, and I never seen or heard from her again. She expressed to my sister that she didn't have time to wait on anyone in prison and that she had a life to live. I couldn't blame her. Did it hurt? Yes. Did I hold a grudge? No. I did it to myself.

This time, instead of being sent to Jackson State Prison, I was sent to Coaster Diagnostic Prison which was close to Savannah, Georgia. That was also one of the longest rides I had ever taken in my life. This time, I was thinking to myself something got to change. I was so sick and tired of going through the same old thing. I went to a drug rehabilitation program and failed. I went to prison and I failed to stay out. I was in a cycle of being in and out of the streets, jail and prison, but was tired of being in this cycle and feeling like a failure.

Chapter 8:
PLAYING WITH GOD

AFTER THE FIRST MONTH OF BEING IN PRISON I decided to go to church. That wasn't an easy decision for me, but I had to try something. I figured that if I gave God a try I might be able to go home. So I started going to church. Two months later I was transferred to River State Prison. The day I stepped off of that bus and looked around I thought I entered a hell hole. The building's windows were blacked out and some appeared to be broken; there was trash all over the place; people were hanging out the windows as they greeted the newcomers. If you ever watched the movie Mad Max, that's what this place resembled to me.

We were escorted into the building. There was a group of guys that were called the CERT Team Officers. These guys stood over you like Andre the Giant. Their arms were as big as my body; their legs the size of a full grown tree. The CERT Team told you what you could and could not do. They escorted us to the building where I had to go through the same ordeal: strip and get searched, degraded, and treated like an animal. They called this "part of the process". They commanded us to get into the shower; afterwards, we were given our prison clothes, lockers for our locker boxes, and our dorm numbers. They then gave us directions to our housing dorms and our bunks—my bunk number was 86.

I left the intake and went to my dorm. As I entered into the dorm, it dawned on me that this would be the place I'd lay my head and call home for the next 7 years. Upon entering the dorm, there was a fight going on. One one guy who stood about 5' 1" and was muscularly built was fighting another guy who stood 6' 2" or 6' 3" and looked like a biker. The short guy's nickname was "Little" and the biker's nickname was "Tiny". I was thinking this has to be a joke.

What started this fight was Tiny mistakenly swung this broom stick at Little, and Little caught the stick handle and broke it; he then ran up on Tiny and wrapped his arms around Tiny's waist as if to pick him up. Tiny began pounding on Little's head with lefts and rights. Those blows seemed to do little damage to Little. Little then bent his knees, tightened his grip around Tiny's waist, and then he began to lift up. All I saw was this short man (Little) holding what looked like a giant (Tiny) up in the air. Suddenly, Little slammed Tiny down to the ground—it sounded like a tree crashing to the ground in a forest. BOOOOM!! That's how loud the thump was when Tiny hit the ground. If you have ever witnessed fire ants covering and attacking their prey before, then you can imagine how it looked when Tiny hit the floor: Little was all over him. Little jumped on Tiny with lightning quickness; he had his arms around Tony's neck and was choking the life out of the big guy. I was literally watching a guy's shade turn from white to pink to purple to dark purple. I watched as life began to escape from a man's eyes. Had an officer not arrived in time, that man (Tiny) would have died right in front of my eyes.

"My God, this is crazy! Why am I here? What is my purpose? I want to go home, but I got seven years of this hell," I thought to myself. The dorm I was in contained 86 people: 86 grown men in one place; 86 bodies; 86 attitudes; 86 crazy people…including myself. "Oh my God! Take me home. Get me the hell away from here! My God!" I thought to myself. Talking to myself, I had to calm myself down: "Okay Steve," I said to myself. "This is your home. This is where you will be staying for the next seven years of your life. You might as well buckle down and get with it. You made your bed, now lie in it. You got to live with these guys. You got to get out of this place. Do what you have to do to survive and go home." I made up in my mind that day that I would survive. I decided that I was going to hold it down like a man and leave out of that place and start my life completely over. I was determined that this was not going to be my destiny.

As time progressed, I began to conform to my surroundings. Sadly, I did not transform my thinking. Mom and dad would send me money. In prison, I learned how to flip the money that was sent to me. I would go to the store and buy a big can of cigarettes and I would roll all of my cigarettes up. I would sell five for soup or five for a stamp—that was money in prison. I would also buy coffee and make what we called "fingers": that's where you would get a glove (plastic or serving glove) and pour coffee down the fingers of the glove; you would then break it off and then twist that finger, and then you would have a coffee bomb—you could sell coffee bombs for soup and stamps. I had to do something with my time, so I sold coffee and cigarettes; but there was still something missing. When I got to River State Prison, I stopped going to church and started to do my own thing instead. I would go outside and work out; I also went to GED class. I would go to the library. I also played dominoes a lot (I thought I was a dominoes champion until I played with my wife. After she whipped me, I stopped playing dominoes).

One weekend, I finally decided to go to church. When I got there, there was no one playing for the choir. I knew how to play the piano, so I decided to work out a deal with the service facilitator. After church, I went to the praise team leader (if that's what you want to call him) and asked him about joining the choir. He said, "Sure you can join the choir, brother."

"Okay. Well, who is playing for you guys?" I asked. He said no one was playing for them. I told him that I could play the piano. He then asked me to demonstrate my skills. I played what I could, and that was all he needed to hear. I was now their new keyboard and piano player. That was my first gig at River State Prison. Hallelujah! The praise team leader told me to come back the next week. When I heard the announcement for the choir to come to rehearsal, I was eager to get down there to the church to play.

When I got to the church, I got on the piano and played. I felt good because I was playing the piano for the church. On Sunday mornings, there was a lady that used to come to the church to speak. She was a powerful minister of the Gospel. She would come some Sunday mornings and some Fridays, and whenever she came to church the church would be packed—everyone came to see this mighty woman of God. One Sunday morning, she came to church and saw me playing the piano. When she got up to preach, she stopped in the middle of her sermon, turned to me and told me to come forward. This was on Father's Day. I will never forget it. She called me up and told me to lift my hands; she then said God told her to bless my hands. She then went and got some oil and put it in her hands, rubbed them together and then intertwined her hands with my hands. From that point on, God began to bless my hands. Wherever I played from that point on, I played under such a powerful anointing from God. But even though I played for the church, I still did not have a relationship with God. God was using me although I didn't know Him. Everything I did was merely for show.

After about a year and a half of being at the Rivers State Prison, I put in for a transfer to go to another prison. I felt like it was time for me to go. I had seen enough there. It was getting too crazy there. After walking into the restroom and stumbling upon two men in the very act, I was now more than ready to go. Believe it or not, when I put in for a transfer to another prison, my request was granted. I was transferred from River State Prison to Troop County, County Camp Down in Lagrange, Georgia, which was very close to home. I was super ecstatic when they told me to pack it up and get ready to relocate to a county camp where you eat good, get to watch more television, get better clothes, and you don't have to deal with overcrowded dorms. This is the next phase just before you are sent to a halfway house, which was my ultimate goal—to get to a halfway house. But there is a process we must undergo before getting to the next phase.

CHAPTER 9:
NEAR DEATH
EXPERIENCE

WHEN I ARRIVED AT THE COUNTY CAMP, I HAD
to work to get myself in position for a transfer. My first detail at Troop County was an
outside detail. Every morning after breakfast, we had to
gear up and head to the red room. Once we got to the red
room, the guards would lock the doors so we couldn't go
back into the building. The only way out was through
the back door, and no one wanted to go out that door
because it was freezing cold out there. Even though our
clothes were a little better than the State Prison clothes,
they weren't sufficient for the winter. The crazy thing is at
Troop County, they had this thing called "the lotto". How
the lotto worked was: you would go out in the cold, hoping that your name would be called so that you could get
on the warm van for detail; if your name wasn't called,
you had to remain on the yard all day until the guys out
on detail returned. That meant you had to eat outside,
use the restroom outside, sleep outside, you had to do

everything outside in the frigid cold or in the sweltering heat under the hot summer sun until the end of the day, which was from 5:30 am until 4:30 pm. So I said to myself, "Self, we got to get from out here!" And I did. The first chance I got I went to the counselor's office to get a detail change. He said to me, "Well, the only place we can send you, Howard, is the kitchen or the laundry room."

"I'll take the kitchen!" I responded.

I knew how to cook a little bit. Momma did teach us how to take care of ourselves. I can cook, sow, clean—you name it. Momma said, "I'm going to make sure you don't have to depend on nobody when you are grown." So my detail was changed from outside to the kitchen. I quickly became the head cook for two shifts. There was nothing to do in the dorms all day, so I decided to spend my time in the kitchen. I had nothing but time on my hands.

2003 was a horrible year for me. I was now going to church and even preaching the Word of God, and because of my musical skills and my ability to teach parts in the choir I was allowed to form a men's choir. The pastor that came to the camp every weekend would teach me as God gave to him, and I, in turn, would teach the Word to my fellow inmates. By being closer to the home, my mother would come and visit me more often. I can still recall in my mind everything leading up to my mother's passing. I, myself, almost died during this tragic time. It was around the 4th of July and we made plans to have a big dinner for the holiday. We ordered stakes, chicken, hamburgers, hot dogs, baked potatoes, salad, ice cream, cake, and drinks. Oh my God, we were going eat good! Everyone couldn't wait for the 4th of July to roll around.

CHAPTER 9: NEAR DEATH EXPERIENCE

There was great expectation in the camp. On the 4th of July I fell sick and nearly died. It all happened so suddenly. I was outside barbecuing. I was standing behind two long huge barbecue grills. I had steaks on one grill and burgers, hot dogs, and chicken on the other grill. Everything was going good until I got bit by a mosquito. That little insect was about to knock a giant off of his feet. I started feeling sicker and sicker by the minute. It became increasingly difficult to do little things like lift my head and open my eyes. The light began to give me an awful headache. I started to feel cold, then hot. When I laid down my head ached, and when I sat up my head ached. I began to vomit. Soon, I found myself vomiting blood. I was rushed to the nurse who examined me and then sent for the transferring official to rush me to the hospital. When I got to the hospital I was examined and then sent back to the camp. This went on for a day and a half until the nurse called the hospital and basically made them admit me.

Once admitted into the hospital, I was given a spinal tap. My diagnosis was that I had viral meningitis, and if they would not have admitted me when they did I would have died that night. After being admitted, I stayed in the hospital two weeks, recovering from my sickness; but the craziest thing happened while I was there: instead of concentrating on getting better, I was more concerned with getting the nurses and doctors phone numbers. Even while on my death bed I was more focused on women than my soul.

After I got well, it was time for me to head back to the camp. I had been living it up in the hospital for the last two weeks and I certainly didn't want to go back, but I had to return back to the land of the living and lost. While I was out sick, the operations of the camp were still going on: visitations on Saturdays and Sundays; detail work every Monday through Friday; church on Wednesdays; practice on Thursdays; the same old, same old. When I got back to the camp I jumped right back into the flow of things; I was right back in the kitchen. Everything was peaceful until one day when we were in the kitchen working a fight broke out in the storage room. Have you ever met someone who loved to talk like he or she was the baddest person on the planet or the one person you'd never want to cross? A person that loves to brag on him or herself? One of my associates/friends who had a lot of mouth was walking around talking about how he wanted to beating up another inmate, a guy who happened to be a quiet person. Apparently, my friend pushed this other guy to his limits. I remember being in the kitchen getting ready for dinner when, all of a sudden, there was a lot of commotion coming from the storage room. When I opened the door to the storage room, all I saw was my friend getting choked out by the quiet guy, the one he had been antagonizing and talking about for the last few weeks. The only thing he (my friend) was able to do was beg someone, "Get him off me! Get him off me! I can't breathe! Get him off me!" The other guy had him in the weasel, attempting to choking the life out of him. For you who do not know what the weasel is, it is when you place one arm under a person's neck and you place your other arm on the back of the person's head and you begin to choke the other person as hard as you can until he or she passes out. In the wrestling ring there are several names for this (Cobra Clutch, etc.), but in prison we called it "the weasel". We reached down and pulled the guys apart. After that, my friend got up and stormed out of the kitchen. He never said anything else to that guy from that day on. Not too long afterwards, I received a visit from my mother. This was one of the saddest times of my life. Somehow, I knew that when she walked into the room (the cafeteria was our visitation room), that would be the last time I would see her alive or at least speak to her while she was still able to communicate. She came and sat down at the table. I grabbed hold of her hand and looked right into her eyes. Something inside of me told me not to let go of her hand. I didn't want to release my mother's hand at any time during her visit. She was telling me about my son, letting me know that he was down in Loganville, Georgia with his aunt and uncle and that he was doing okay. She informed me that Bishop (that's what she always called my dad) was at home lying down and that he sent his hello and told me to come on home soon. But I couldn't shake that nagging sense that I would never again see my mother alive. I knew it. I felt it. God was letting me know it. I refused to let go of her hands while we sat and talked. One of the officers came over to me and said,

"You must really love your girlfriend here."
I smiled at him, looked my mother, and said, "Yeah, I love her so much." Our visit lasted for another three hours. Suddenly, an officer stood up and said,

"Visitation is over! You must leave now!"

That day I felt as if my heart would leave my chest. My mom got up, and then we hugged. I remember watching her as she headed towards the door to leave the facility. Once she got to the door, she turned around and then looked at me; somehow, that look confirmed to me that I would never see her alive again. She then turned around and walked out of the door. I dragged myself out the visitation room and went to the shakedown room to be searched. This was necessary to make sure that no inmates were carrying anything back into the prison from their visitations. I felt so numb because of the heart wrenching feeling in my gut which said that was my last visitation from my mother.

It wasn't too long after my mother's last visitation that I received a letter from home that read:

"Stephen, how are you doing? I pray all is well. I am doing fine but mom is in the hospital. She's having a hard time breathing. Nobody knows what is going on. The doctor cannot pinpoint the problem and everyone is baffled. They are trying everything to get her to breathe normally. The doctor has tried so many different types of medicine but nothing seemed to work. She can inhale but she cannot exhale." Grace

Mom was inhaling oxygen, but she could not exhale the carbon monoxide. We knew that the carbon monoxide was poisoning her.

When I read those words I began to worry, cry, and pray. "I knew it! I knew it!" I said to myself. I became angry with God. Why? Because, when I was being sentenced to prison the last time, I prayed a specific

100

prayer to God. I asked, "God, please don't take my mother away while I am gone these seven years. Please let her see me come home." Now, I was hearing the news that she was on her deathbed and couldn't breathe. I felt like God did not listen to me; I felt I wasn't good enough for Him to pay attention to, I wasn't good enough to be heard. I cried out to God, "I read the Bible! I know you hear everyone else! Why can't you hear me? My momma... Why can't she breathe?! Why you got to take her?! Why you can't answer my prayer?! You answered Abraham's prayer. Why can't you answer my prayer?! You answered Isaac's prayer. Why can't you answer my prayer?! You answered Jacob's prayer. Why can't you answer my prayer?! Jesus, can't you hear what I'm saying?!" I cried out to God. As time went by, my brother, father, sister, and everyone that I called gave me false hope—everyone except for one of my brothers who kept it real with me. Everyone else led me to believe that my mother was going to be alright. Perhaps, they were in denial: they so desperately wanted momma to live that they didn't want to accept the possibility of her passing away. But I had it hard because I had to face the possibility of losing my mother while in prison, unable to be by her side. Everyday, I would call home. Everyday, the news would grow more negative. Finally, the day that I dreaded for so long came. I remember it like it was yesterday.

CHAPTER 10:
THE DAY I STOPPED BELIEVING

My body was there in that dorm, but my mind was at home with momma. Suddenly, my name was called over the loud speaker: "Stephen Howard! Report to the counselor's office!" No one in prison wants to hear that call. The only an inmate wants to hear their name called like that over the intercom is when they know they are about to go home. When I arrived to the counselor's office, the counselor was sitting behind his desk. When I entered into his office he stood up, came out from behind his desk, grabbed my hand and then said,

"I have some terrible news that I have to tell you."

I braced myself to face the bad news, to hear him tell me that my mother had passed on to the other side. I wasn't quite sure how I would take the news. I always told myself that if my mom died while I was in prison I was going to go crazy, or that I was going to try to escape. I had all kinds of thoughts going through my mind. The counselor took my hand and said, "I have some news for you; however, your sister is on the phone and I want her to speak to you." I picked up the phone and my oldest sister, Catherine, was on the phone. She said,

"Steve, momma is gone."

At first, things weren't registering in my mind. I could not believe that my mother was gone. I couldn't believe that God did not honor my prayer request. All of my emotions went away. I went numb. When the realization of what had happened finally did hit me, it hit me like a tsunami. I immediately broke down. I broke down because the woman that I called my best friend, the woman that gave birth to me, the one that I was able to go everything that was going on in me with, the one that I was able to talk to when I was not able to talk to anyone else, the one that knew me like no one else, the one that I loved dearly with all my heart, mind, soul, and spirit was gone. When the news hit me I wondered what I was going to do and who was I going to turn to? I felt that I had no one else in the world that I could confide in. There seemed to be no one else in the world that I could turn to, no one else in the world that I trusted like my mother; no one.

I never asked God "why" after my momma passed. "Oh God!" was the only thing that I could say. "Oh God, mom is gone!" A person who has never lost their mother would fully understand how I felt. If your mother is still with you, cherish her, cherish the time that you have with her...and your father because they are precious.

I cried until I had no more tears to cry. I got up,

left the counselor's office, and went into the hall where the prisoners were roaming. Some noticed that I was up-set and others (the ones I associated with) came over to console me, but I was seemingly in a daze. My mind was still trying to process the news I had just received. I still couldn't believe that my mother was gone and I was there of all places in a God forsaken prison. That darn judge could have gave me 3 years instead of a 20 year sentence. She could have given me time served I was thinking. As those thoughts moved through my mind I grew even more upset with God. "You was supposed to be so pow-erful, supposed to be so mighty! You supposed to be all of this and that! Everything I saw coming up as a little child—you healed people! I know you did because you did it for my daddy. You raised people from the dead—I know you did because I saw you do it when I was a child. So, why couldn't you do this one little thing for me? Why did you choose to ignore me? Was I not important to you? What? Were you so busy that you did not have time to listen to me? I love my momma, too! I need my momma, too! What was I going to do now? Who could I call on now? You never been there for me when I was out there smoking dope! You wasn't there for me when I was out there by myself! You wasn't there for me when I was cold outside and nobody wanted to take me in! You wasn't there for me!" I said to God. Oh I was mad and I wanted to be heard. I wanted God to know exactly how I felt. I believed that I had the right to feel this way. I truly believed that I was the victim there. I truly believed that I was entitled to have whatever I wanted. While fussing at God it never dawned on me that I was the cause for ev-erything that I was going through; that it was my actions and decisions in life that landed me in that prison, not God; it was my insistence on living the way I was living in those streets that ripped me away from my family. I forgot about all of the times God answered my prayers, even intervening and blocking me from receiving prison time when I should have just so that I would have the opportunity to be with my family, friends, and loved ones. I was only thinking about myself, but not considering my own responsibility and role in the circumstances I was facing. I didn't even think about the fact that I wasn't the only one praying for momma and going through. All I thought about was the fact that momma was dead and God did not do what I wanted Him to do and that I now felt all alone. Today, I know that I was very selfish. I was selfish to blame God and not look at my own actions. I was selfish enough to think God owed me an answer and was supposed to do what I wanted Him to do. I had the audacity to question God because of His decision to call my mother home.

I went back to my dorm, jumped on the phone, and called home, looking to speak to my father. When he came to the phone, I could hear him on the other end crying. "Daddy?"

"Yes, son."

"How are you feeling?"

"I don't know. I was praying and I began to ask God, 'Why did you take my wife from me? Why did you take her? Why did you not take me?' And as I was talking to God and asking him why he took my wife, God said to me 'Why not? I took Eve from Adam; I took Sarah from Abraham; what makes you so different that I cannot take Lovillar from you?'"

The sound of him breaking down crying caused my heart to break. I realized I wasn't the only one going through—my father was going through real bad; after all, my father and mother had been married for 60 years.

After my conversation with my dad I went back to my bunk with a heavy heart. I began to reflect back over my childhood with my parents; I did this while rocking myself to sleep. I didn't eat anything that day, nor the next morning. I ate around lunchtime, though. I found the strength to embrace my new reality after hearing a voice say to me, "Let the dead bury the dead. Life goes on." That didn't change the fact that I was still mad at God, though. But at least I still desired to go to church. I still had responsibilities to handle. One Sunday, Pastor Burks, who was my pastor at the time, and I sat down and talked. I told him everything that happened to me. He shared with me these words: "I know, son. I heard about it. I've been praying for you the whole time." Those words gave me strength.

After accepting the passing of my mother, my next step was to go to the funeral. Prior to her passing, I was asked by the camp's facilitators if I wanted to go to the hospital to be by my mother's side or simply wait until after she has passed and then go to the funeral. I didn't feel it necessary to go and stay at the hospital since my brothers and sisters were feeding me false hope by claiming momma was going to survive. Had I known the truth, I would have chosen to remain by her bedside at the hospital much sooner than I did. By the time I got to the hospital to see my mother, she was barely responsive; but I knew she could still hear me, though. I began to sing for her one of the songs she used to love to hear me sing, a song that I wrote: "What you gonna do when judgment come for you."

After singing her favorite song, I grabbed her hand and said, "Momma, I got something that I want to tell you." Then I bent over, looked into her face, and said, "Momma, I got your name tattooed on my chest." At that, she tried to raise herself up in the bed, though she never opened her eyes. I knew she was angry over that. I then gently pushed her back down in the bed and reassured her, "It's okay. It's okay, mom. It's okay." I told her that I wasn't going to get anymore tattoos (which was a lie. I got several more tattoos after that for a total of 13 tattoos in all). I am grateful for those final moments because I didn't even get a chance to go to her funeral. I got put on lockdown in my dorm until after the funeral.

By this time, I no longer worked in the kitchen. My detail was in the administrative office. I was working around the warden, the secretary, and the accountants. My detail was to keep the supply room in order and to make sure the office stayed clean. Basically, I was a custodian. I enjoyed being in that position. My detail gave me more freedom to roam around in the prison. No one else in the prison had as much freedom as I did. I was not constantly on lockdown. If I wasn't at work, I was either at church or doing something productive. I didn't like sitting inside of a dorm all day looking at television. I remained in the County Camp for another year before being transferred to the Atlanta Transition Center, which was located on Ponce de Leon Avenue in downtown Atlanta, Georgia. Now, I was right around the corner from our house. I could basically look out my window and see my neighborhood.

CHAPTER 11:
TRICKS ARE FOR KIDS

MY LIFE WAS ABOUT TO MAKE AN AWESOME turn. During this time in my life, I began to transition back into society. I did four years in prison, and this was my last three years to do. There's no better place to spend your prison time than in a transitional center. I no longer had to wear prison clothes; I wore clothes like everyone else in the free world. The doors to this center were never locked. On certain days we were allowed to go to Krogers. We were able to keep money in our pocket. I was able to buy ice cream, go to the vending machine, eat whatever I wanted to eat as opposed to that nasty, horrible prison food that was served every morning and every evening. I was able to do what I wanted to do. I was basically free. When I got to the transition center I was given a work detail: I was assigned to the kitchen, which is where I didn't want to be. I preferred to be in another kitchen. I had heard so much about the kitchen downtown at the GBA building—that's the kitchen I wanted to bake in. I was on a mission. I had a goal of owning my own business once I got out. I was a baker by trade; I desired to perfect this skill; in order for me to do so, I had to put myself in a position that would truly allow me to perfect my skills. I worked in the kitchen at the Transitional Center for about a month, then I applied for the kitchen in the GBA building. "Permission granted. Detail change: Stephen Howard, report downstairs to receive your clothes." I went downstairs and got four white pairs of pants, four white shirts, aprons, some boots, a belt, a baker's hat, and instructions on what and what not to do.

When I first got to GBA, everything was running good. I quickly picked up on baking and became one of GBA's best bakers. I baked cakes and pies all morning from scratch—nothing came out of a box. Everything that I made—every cake, pie, cobbler, pound cake, etc.— would sell out. Banana pudding, peach cobbler, potato pie, apple pie, apple cobbler, strawberry cake, German chocolate cake, red velvet cake, Oreo dirt cake, carrot cake—it didn't matter. Whatever I made, it always sold out. I got so good at baking that, not only was I baking for GBA, but I was now baking for number 2 Peachtree St. and 244 Washington St. Instead of baking for one restaurant, every morning I was baking for three restaurants and I was making my quarters. I was ready to start my own business now, but I still had one problem: I will still in prison. I became the senior prisoner at GBA, and people began to look to me for guidance; I had to show them how to do certain things. I even trained two guys on how to bake cakes and pies. But there was one officer that did not like me. I suspected he didn't like me because a great deal of women at GBA found me interesting. Perhaps, it was due to the fact that some of those women would speak to me. Maybe it was the fact that even his ex-girlfriend took interest in me. I don't know. What do you think? What I did know is he had it out for me. With his position and my position being what they were, he had the upper hand on me. But, interestingly enough, God still looked after me and granted me favor even though I didn't know Him. To make a long story short, on one particular day, while I was uploading images of a few cakes and pies online, a woman that he was crazy about came down into the cafeteria to get lunch. She spoke to me and I spoke back. He saw us speaking and smiling at one another, and while we were in the midst of having a conversation he angrily got up, came over to me, and said, "Leave her alone!"

"Man, I don't want her. Evidently, she don't want you. Man, you walking behind her like a little puppy," I responded quite demonstrably—I was imitating a whining puppy while telling him that. That lit a fire under his behind. I wish I had never said one thing to that power-abusing officer. I should have kept my mouth shut, but I didn't. In turn, he decided to tell a lie on me. He went and told Ms. Kane, who was the Director over the whole detail at GBA, that I was flirting with the women at GBA. One of the main rules at GBA was that we were not to conversate with the women there. Ms. Kane came to me and asked me if I was talking to one particular woman: the officer's ex-girlfriend. I told her yes, but explained that it was she who spoke to me first. She reminded me that we were not to talk to the customers. I then said "Yes, ma'am" and then left it alone. As far as I was concerned, that was the end of that. But Ms. Kane began acting differently towards me. While I would be cooking, baking, and talking to others (particularly, those I was instructed not to talk to), I would noticed her standing at a distance observing everything I was doing. The creepy feeling that I was being watched was ever present. It got so bad that I became very uncomfortable and just wanted to get the heck away from there. But I was on a mission, I had a goal, I had a vision, and I was determined to see it come true. As time progressed, Ms. Kane's intentions became more pronounced: she wanted me to go back to prison. I realized that if I were to slip up just one time, they would have a reason to send me back to prison.

I can recall in one instance, while I was absent, some of the guys back in the kitchen area were making a lot of noise; they were dancing and carrying on like they were in a club. It was told to me that the customers were hearing this noise. Ms. Kane immediately went into the kitchen and took the radio they allowed us to use, and then she got on everyone back there. However, the interesting thing is this: despite the fact that I wasn't even there that day, I got blamed for what happened. The next morning, when I went into the kitchen, I noticed that a meeting was already in session between Ms. Kane and the workers. I joined in the meeting. When I joined in, she began to say, "There are some of you that have been here longer than anybody else. You think that because you been here the longest, you can do anything you want to do. Well, I got news for you: I will send your butt back to prison so fast it'll make your head swim…. faster than you can shake a stick. If you think I'm going to let you run this place, you better think again." The whole time she was talking she was looking in my direction; her eyes even met mine. I then said to myself,

"WOW! Now that I know you got it out for me, I got to get away from this place."

I had one true ally at GBA: Mrs. Dorothy Woods (we'd call her Miss Dot). This woman would pray for us and counsel us whenever we needed her to. She was our angel; she was my angel in that place. She really helped me get through this time, especially considering that I felt as if I was tiptoeing around in a snake bed everyday. In order for me to get out and start my own business I had to work my way through this. Everything seemed to be going according to plan—according to my plan, not God's.

I got up every morning, got dressed, got on the van, reached my detail, and started cooking. On Saturdays, some of us were allowed to go to GBA to help them prepare for banquets that were going on at night; but while the others were preparing for banquets, I would prepare cakes and pies for the upcoming week. I was doing dirt, too, in that I would have people come up to GBA to bring me money that I wasn't suppose to have and when I didn't go to GBA on Saturday I received my visits. I had one young lady that was crazy about me— anything I asked her to do she would do it. We didn't even have sex, yet; but I had her mind wrapped around my finger. She would come to visit me when I wasn't on detail. She would bring me money, creatine pills, and anything else I asked for (anything but drugs). I didn't want that stuff. I did not want to see drugs. My interest was in other things. Sadly, God was not one of them. I still held animosity towards God. I was even, at that point, willing to sell my soul to the devil, but I figured even he didn't really care to take me; so, I was like "F*** the both of God and the devil." It was all about me then: my will, my desires, my way, my plans.

My primary focus was on getting out of prison—getting my life back was my goal. As time drew closer for me to be transferred to unit 2, I worked diligently and very hard; I did so until it was time for me to transition from a detail to an actual job. I could finally go out and get a job. "Oh man, this was going to be great," I thought into myself. But then, Ms. Kane came to me and offered me the job at GBA. "You can't be serious," I thought. One day, while in the kitchen at GBA, I was approached by a guy named Joe who was one of the cooks. He came to me inquiring about what Ms. Kane asked me. I told him she asked me to work at the GBA—"Man, you're not going to believe that: she asked me if I wanted to be a cook here in this place. I told her no, and that I already had a job waiting for me." But I didn't. I lied. I did not have a job waiting for me, but I refused to work at GBA.

When it was time for me to move to the "working phase" in the transition center, my first job was at Cow Tipper. This was a place that you had to be open minded to work at to say the least. I stayed at Cow Tipper for about a month before being fired. After I got fired from there, I went back to the transitional center—at the center, they had this little kangaroo court we would have to attend if we got into any trouble; so I had to go to court. While there, I explained to the officials why I got fired from my job. When I entered the room, there were three counselors and the center director there waiting for me. They began questioning me about the incident that took place on my job. I told them what happened. They looked at me and, wearing their judgmental attitudes on their faces, they said, "Your punishment is no weekend pass, and you are to return to the kitchen for detail for a month." Upon receiving the punishment, I was confused, mad and upset. I was angry at this whole situation. While walking back to my room, I began to think to myself,

"Self, I got to find a way to go home. If I can't go on the weekends, it's gotta be another way."

I was back at the transitional center over the next 30 days, baking cornbread and cakes and hating every minute of it. But during this time, I came up with a plan that would allow me to go home, and I knew that it would work. At the end of the first week in the center I was called to the counselor's office. "Come in and have a seat, Stephen. We know you are a baker and Ms. Kane want you to come out to GBA until you are able to go back to work," the counselor said.

"Oh hell naw" I said to myself. "This is the last thing I need right now. This has to be a set-up to send me back to prison. This is all she (Ms. Kane) needs," I was thinking to myself while the counselor was talking. After being told that I was being sent back to GBA for detail, I zoned out; the counselor's voice began to sound like the teacher from Charlie Brown: "Wan, wan, wan, wan,wan,wan."

"Ok, I can do this," I said to myself while leaving the office. I just had to bite the bullet, toughen up, and get the heck out of there. I won't lie and say it was easy for me to do that. Those 30 day were the worst I ever spent in prison. I caught more hell than ever.

When the 30 days were over, it was time for me to go out and get another job. I came up with a plan to find a job as far away from the transitional center as possible. I was determined to get home one way are another. I found a job at Publix downtown in the Buckhead community, which was far away from the transitional center. I just knew that the officials were not going to drive all the way out there to see if I was at work. Also, to put the icing on the cake, the position was a night position. "OH MAN!!!!! I got it made now. I beat you! Haa!!! I beat you! Telling me I can't go home. I'll show you! I'll go home anytime I choose and you can't stop me!" I thought to myself. But little did I know I was setting myself up for a crash landing.

CHAPTER 12:
TWO-FACED ADDICTION

I WAS ALWAYS VERY GOOD WITH NUMBERS. I WOULD play the Georgia lottery Cash 3 and would hit the number three, sometimes four times a week. I was just that good, but I had one problem: I couldn't keep that kind of money on me while at the center. One Wednesday, I went too far; to tell you the truth, it was out of control. That day, I did my thing with the numbers: I made a phone call and told the person on the other end what numbers to play. When it was time for the numbers to come out, I went to my television and, lo and behold, my number hit!!!! I was as happy as a kid around Christmas time. I rushed to the phone and called the person who played the number for me. When he answered, he asked me what I wanted him to do. I gave him another number to play and told him I would meet him somewhere to pick up my money. He said okay. He did as I asked and played the next number, which was also a winner. My mind was now running 1000 miles per hour. Every since I started working at Publix I would, on my breaks and lunch period, go to the Dick's Sporting Goods Store and window shop. One day, I saw a pair of tennis shoes that I wanted. They cost over $100. I would tell myself that I was going to buy those shoes just as soon as I got the money. And now that I had the money, I was going to get those shoes. Excitedly, I got up and got myself ready to meet the guy and get my money. I always thought of myself as a pretty boy; I had to look the part even while at the transitional center. I had five holes in my ears and wore earrings in both ears. Every night, after leaving the center, I'd put my earrings in my ears. But on one particular night things were about to change. My earrings were about to get me in a bunch of trouble; they were going to be my downfall.

I was heading to work. On my way to work I called the guy and told him where to meet me. I told him to meet me at a Waffle House. When I arrived there, the guy was waiting for me. We started counting out the money. It was $500 for me. As he counted out the money, my heart began to pound in my chest and I got this queasy, sick feeling in the pit of my stomach—a warning before destruction. But then, I began to focus on those shoes and forgot about the warning. After getting my money, I went to work that night happy, but for some reason, I just couldn't shake the queasiness in my stomach. After I finished my shift, it was time for me to clock out and go back to the center. After clocking out, I went straight to Dick's Sporting Goods Store to get those tennis shoes. But when I got there they didn't have any left in stock. I was stuck with a ton of money on me that I had to spend that night because I couldn't afford to get caught with it on me at the center lest I risk going back to prison. But what was I going to spend it on? I didn't want to just spend it on anything. I was allowing my taste to outweigh my commonsense in that moment, something that would in turn send me back to prison.

Since Dick's Sporting Goods didn't have what I wanted, I went over to the Finer Basement Store, which was a high end thrift store in Buckhead. I figured that was a good place to spend that cash. The only thing I found there was a very bright, high yellow Polo shirt. After leaving the store, I went over to Lenox Square mall. I still wanted to find those tennis shoes. I didn't have any success at the mall. I tried another sports wear store, but found no luck there either. Time was running out. So, I decided to just get a pair of shoes—any pair, as long as they were in style. I was waiting on someone to assist, but they were moving very slow. I began to feel disrespected due to their not giving me any attention; after all, time was running out and I had to hurry up and get back to the center; I was in a rush. Noticing what appeared to be store workers just loafing around taking their dear sweet time, I left the store and went to Macy's Department Store. Immediately, I received assistance from a sales person. I explained to the sales person what I was looking for. He said, "You are in luck. We just got some new Reeboks in today. You might like." We proceeded forward. He took my foot measurement and then went to get the shoes. The second I laid my eyes on them I was ready to buy them. They were originally priced at $108, but were on sale for $75.

After buying the shoes and heading back to the center, I was faced with the challenge of figuring out how to get my money and my new shoes and shirt back into the center. Had the facilitators discovered that I'd been shopping I knew they'd send me back to prison. I began to think about what I could do. While on Marta (public transportation), I came up with what I thought was a master plan on how I would sneak my merchandise into the center. I was confident that this would work. The train passed the Five Points Train Station and was headed to my stop: the North Avenue Train Station. I had a little pep in my step now because I knew that I had it all worked out. It's interesting that the same mentality I had when I was out in the streets was the same mentality I operated in while in prison. When I got off at the North Avenue Train Station my bus was not there, so I walked around the train station to the other side to speak to a friend of mine who was always there selling drinks, cigarettes, hats, water, shades, and more. This guy was in a wheelchair. We had become good friends by now. I would come and see him every day on my way home from work. I remember telling him that I was trying to hit the big number in the Georgia lottery, and I promised him that if I hit it I was going to return to him and pretty much buy everything that he had. So, this was the day—I had hit the lottery. I didn't hit the big number, but I had enough money in my pocket to buy some stuff from him. When I ran into my friend I said, "Didn't I tell you I was coming back, man? Boy, I hit the Cash 3 two days in a row, and, boy, I'm straight. I got some money. I need to spend it with you." We were happy to see each other. I bought some things from him and we talked for a little while. I then told him that I had to go because my bus should be back on the other side of the train station. We said our goodbyes and then I walked back to the other side of the train station. I waited for about three minutes when suddenly my bus pulled up. When the bus stopped two of my roommates got off the bus. I asked them who was on duty at the center and they said "Sergeant." I knew then that I really had to hide my money because Sergeant was the type of person that would search you the moment you arrived at the center, and if he found any extra money on you he would keep it for himself. I was determined not to let him take my money. I was so concerned about not losing my money that I forgot to take out my earrings before returning to the center.

I got on the bus thinking mainly about my money. When I arrived at the transition center I pulled the stopping cord, got off the bus, and then noticed the details van pulled up across the street and those who worked on detail at GBA getting on it. I then hollered from across the street, "Hey! Hey! Hey!" But they did not hear me. I then ran across the street and headed to my unit: unit two. As I walked up the sideway heading for unit two, Sergeant came through the door.

"What's up, Sarge," I said.

At first he looked and said "hey," but then he took a double look. Something caught his attention. I suddenly realized what he was looking at and immediately held my hand up to my ears. I knew I was screwed. "Give them to me," he said. I took my earrings out of my ears and put them in his hand, and while handing them over to him he looked down at my feet and said, "Those new shoes, aren't they?"

"No, Sarge. I been had these.

"Boy, I think you been shopping. Come on in here and let me shake you down." At that point, I knew I was done. We went inside unit two and where there was another officer sitting behind the intake/out-take booth. "Guess what?" Sergeant addressed the other officer.

"What?" she responded.

"Howard been shopping," he told her. She then looked at me, shocked, and said,

"Howard?!!!"

I had nothing to say. Sergeant then told me to open my bag, which I did. The officers then pulled out my bright yellow Polo shirt. I mean, this thing was so bright it brightened up the whole room! Now, you have to understand that in prison and in the transitional center everything is dull: the walls are dull, the furniture is dull, the carpet is dull; everything is gloomy and designed to keep you in a depressed state. So, something as bright as that yellow shirt in prison is like a ray of sunshine—the darkness cannot handle the light. After searching through my bag, Sergeant asked me where I was coming from. I told him I was just getting off of work. He then instructed the other officer to call my job to see what time I got off of work. I didn't think to cover all of my ends in this grand master plan of mine. All I began to think about at this point was getting to my room so that I could hurry up and hide my money—perhaps, stuff it inside of one of my letters or in my paperwork. I figured that I was too deep in trouble and was possibly going back to prison that night. Remember when I told you I had a queasy feeling in my stomach earlier that day?

A few minutes later, I was called to the office. Sergeant asked me what happened. By then, I had enough time to think of a good lie. But apparently, my lie wasn't convincing enough. The officers then told me to go to my room. A few minutes later they called me back down to the office and told me to put my hands on the counter. I was searched to see if I had any contraband on my person. After that I was escorted to the shipping hole. They then brought me some prison clothes and told me to change into my prison gear. And there I was, going to the hole. I never been in the hole before, but there's a first for everything.

After being sent to the hole, the next thing I knew I was on a van heading back to Jackson State Prison. When I arrived, I was placed in a holding cell. Prior to this unfortunate chain of events I was a vegetarian, but when they put me in the hole I quickly started eating meat. It was either eat what they give you or starve. I stayed in this cell for about two weeks before being sent to my new home: Walker State Prison, which was way up in the north Georgia mountains. It was a good little ride. When we finally arrived there, I got off of the van and looked up at the sky, which seemed to be so close I felt like I could touch it with my hand. "Oh man, where in the hell have they brought me to?" I murmured to myself. An officer approached us, escorted us inside the prison, gave us our new belongings, and then sent us to our cells. When I entered the cell house one of the inmates directed me to my bunk. I don't know if you've ever seen a three-bunk-high bed before; well, they have them in prison. My bunk was so high up I could have gotten a nose bleed.

CHAPTER 13:
YOU NEVER LEARN

I CLIMBED UP TO MY BUNK, SAT BACK, AND TOOK A look at my surroundings, and then thought to myself, "Man, I was just basically free. I had money in my pocket, I was eating what I wanted, I had a girl that I was seeing most nights, and I was going home whenever I wanted. Now look at me! Man, this sucks. IT SUCKs!!!!!" All I could do was suck it up and make the best of it. At least I only had four months before I could go home. "Hey!!! I can do this," I thought to myself. "Heck, I can do that standing on my head." I was quickly moved to the fast track part of the prison, down at the bottom of the prison camp. The fast track is a part of the prison that is set aside for those who have less than six months of prison time left to serve. Everyone in the fast track had to go out on detail. I had the pleasure of working in the prison warehouse. Everything—and I do mean EV-ERYTHING—passed through the warehouse. We had first pick on everything! While on that particular detail assignment, I had the opportunity to teach myself how to use sign language and also study the CDL Driving

Manual. I figured that if I knew how to operate a tractor trailer when I got out, then I'd be alright. I figured that a CDL was a black man's ticket out of the ghetto. And by now, I was determined more than ever to not be just another statistic.

Those four months went by real quick. Before I knew it, I was being released. YES!!!! I was finally going home. I served over seven years in prison and didn't plan on going back. When I got home I called my brother to see where he was—I had given him the authority to get all of my earnings from my job while I was at the transitional center. Now, I needed my money. I went to my room to search for my belongings, which Calvin, my brother, kept there for me after I was last sent back to prison. I found my money he stashed away for me and then immediately set out to look for a job driving trucks. Reality set in very quickly as I was rejected by every job I applied for. Every trucking company I called informed me in so many words that they were not looking to hire someone with my background. It didn't even matter if I had my CDL or not. After this, I called my brother, mad, upset, sad and disappointed, crying like a big baby. I was crying because all of my dreams seemed to be flying out of the window, and I had no net available to catch them with before they completely escaped my grasp. Everything I had hope for and every ounce of faith in myself was vanishing quickly. "Why is it so hard?!" I cried. "I'm trying to do what's right! Why can't they give people that been to prison another chance?! Why are they always holding our past over our heads? I don't know! I don't know! I don't know!! What am I going to do? I'm tired! I'm tired!! I'm tired!!! I keep searching for a job and nobody wants to give me a chance! I mean, I'm trying to change! I want to do right! Why won't they give me a chance?!"

"I know, bro," my brother responded. "I know. Just hold on, brah. You going to make it, man! You going to do good. You just got to hold on, okay? Don't lose your faith."

"FAITH!!!" I thought. "Man, what's faith?! Man, get out of my face talking bout some d*** faith!! What faith ever done for me, huh?!! Nothing!! Absolutely nothing!!!" Going through my mind was the death of my mother—I didn't want to hear about anything that referred to God.

After my conversation with my brother I resumed searching for a job. I called different companies but they all said the same thing. One company said the only way I would drive a truck would be in construction, hauling raw materials, which really wasn't my dream, my vision for myself. What in the hell are you talking about—raw materials? I'll show you! That was my mentality. "I'm going to prove you wrong. I'm going to prove everyone wrong. I don't want to haul no dirt, no rocks, no raw materials; I want to drive a rig! I want to be a real truck driver. My brothers drive, my nephew drive; it's in the family. I got to be a driver," I said. "I don't have nobody to be responsible for. I want to be a road driver." I insisted that this would be my destiny although God had other plans in store for me.

I didn't know why, but I knew that I didn't want to drive a dump truck. I still thought of myself as a pretty boy, as someone too handsome to get dirty. I figured I needed to operate a rig. But there was one tiny problem:

I never drove a truck before in my life. I studied and took the test to get my class A and class B permits and my license to operate a dump truck and a rig, but I had never driven either of them. After regaining my composure, I thought about the steps I needed to take in order to reach my goal: first, I needed to learn how to actually operate a truck, so I went to a temporary staffing company and applied for a job driving a box truck. I figured that if I learned how to drive a box truck then driving a big truck wouldn't be a problem.

The temporary agency got me a job driving for Wheeler Windows and Doors. I worked for Wheeler for a while. My job description was to deliver windows and doors to different communities and office complexes that were under construction. We delivered windows, doors, baseboard, roof trimming, attic stairs—things of that nature. It was a very strenuous job. None of the Wheeler trucks had air conditioning, so we had to work in the blazing hot summer heat with our windows down. There were many times that I would find myself lost. I didn't know how I ended up in Kalamazoo, Georgia, nor how I ended up in Buggtussle, Georgia.

This wasn't the job I wanted initially, but it's the one that I settled for. Why? Because it was available to me and it was a step towards reaching my goal. One day, while at work I nearly died. I had to make a delivery up in the Lake Arrowhead Mountain going towards Jasper, Georgia (towards Big Canoe Mountain). My first time going up in the mountains was very frightening for me because I never been that high up before, especially in a truck. I also have a slight fear of heights. While we were riding up the mountain I looked over the edge and noticed I couldn't see the bottom. Still, I continued to go up the mountain. I grew more and more comfortable the higher we got. While driving, we ended up getting lost— trust me, you never want to get lost in the mountains. To top it all off, it started to drizzle. This caused the road to become dangerous to drive on. I thought I was going in the right direction, but I was actually on the wrong side of the mountain; so I had to turn that big box truck around and go in the other direction. This was where the problem began. This was where I began to think twice about becoming a trucker driver. I was going down a hill. At the connecting street at the bottom of that hill was a cliff. When I got to the connecting street I turned to my right upon noticing some homes in that direction—although there were a few houses on the street to my left as well. When I came upon the homes I noticed that the addresses did not match my order sheet, so I began to back away from that area. While backing up and moving towards the other houses that were on the other street, but they weren't the right location either. I then put the truck in first gear and headed back up the hill, and that's when it got crazy. I was going up the hill slowly when, all of a sudden, the truck started to bounce; it went "boom, boom, boom, boom." Then the stick shift popped out of gear. My mind started to race after that because when the truck popped out of gear it started to go backwards real fast. The first thought that came to my mind was to jump out of the truck, which was heading straight for the cliff. I looked to my right and my rider was looking at me with fear-filled eyes. He reached towards me as if to say 'don't leave'. The next thought that popped into my mind was to turn the steering wheel to my right. I began to turn that steering wheel. It was difficult to turn, but I turned it like I was turning it for my life—which I was. Miraculously, it was as if someone picked up the truck and placed it in a yard that was to our left, which shouldn't have happened according to logic and the way and speed in which the truck was moving towards that cliff. But that truck was now heading towards one of the houses to our left while moving full speed ahead—heading towards someone's front door. It dawned on me just in time to pull the emergency brakes; when I did, the truck stopped just a few inches away from someone's front door. Once the truck was stopped, I jumped out; my heart was in my shorts. I was breathing heavily while pointing at the truck and saying, "You… You… You…" When I circled around the truck I noticed that somehow a tree was bent under the truck. "When in the hell did that happen?" I asked. After all of this happened, I got on my phone and I called the warehouse to let them know what happened and that I needed someone to come and get the truck. I had no plans of getting back in that truck nor any other truck as far as I was concerned. But the dispatcher informed me that it was my responsibility, my duty to bring back their truck. So I had to toughen up, put my big boy pants on, get back in that truck and drive it up that hill, deliver my drop and then get my butt back to the warehouse. So I got back in the truck, backed it out of that yard, backed down the street to the hill, and then backed that truck up the hill all while looking at the cliff that stood before me. When I got to the top of the hill, my rider jumped in the truck and we drove all the way to the other side of the mountain, delivered the materials, got back in the truck, and got out of there and back to the warehouse. When

CHAPTER 13: YOU NEVER LEARN

I got back to the warehouse I told them what happened and explained that I had no intentions on going back to the mountains. I was fine with driving on flat land. No more mountains.

The job was okay. I grew accustomed to the operations of the company. I was usually one of the first to arrive there every morning and one of the last to leave every evening. But sadly, the company began to lose several of its million dollar contracts, which resulted in them having to let people go. Drivers were now being laid off. Interestingly enough, perhaps it was due to my work ethics that I was among the last drivers to be let go.

At Wheeler I was doing pretty good. I was making a decent pay check every week. I had money in my pocket. Also, I met two women: the first one I liked for her body, but the second one had more of my attention because she had a banging body and an outstanding mind. She was about seven years older than me, though. But when I got with her, my life began to change.

CHAPTER 14:
BEER AND SPIRITS

THE FIRST WOMAN I MET AT A WAL-MART ON Panola Road and the second one I met at a liquor store off of Wesley Chapel. The second one was more memorable because she had a greater impact in my life. She was in the liquor store looking very good. You know I had to put my old max daddy tired pimp game into effect. Noticing that she was having an unpleasant experience at the counter, I strolled over, invaded her space, and gave her the lamest line I could think of: "Excuse me miss, I don't see no wedding ring on your finger. I was wondering is it possible that I can get your name and number?" The way she looked at me was as if to say Nigga, get the hell out of my face!! I felt like a fool. I left the store and got in my car—I was driving a Black 2009 Dodge Charger; it was as clean as my head after a fresh shave in the morning. While sitting in my car she came out the store. I glanced her way but refused to say another word. A minute later, I was startled by a knock on my window. It was her. I rolled down the window and she asked me my name. I gave her my name and she gave me hers. Then she said,

"You gonna come up to me with that tired line." I smiled and said,

"You look so classy I was lost for words."

"Oh, now, that's good. I was telling my daughter about you just now, and she pushed me to talk to you. What's your number," she asked. I looked at her and noticed she didn't have a pencil or paper in her hand.

"Don't you need something to write with?" I asked.

"No. I can remember it. I have a good memory," she replied. So I gave her my number and she asked me to get out of the car so that she could introduce me to her daughter and her dog, which I did. After that we said our goodbyes and I left feeling myself.

I scooped myself up an older woman. "I'm gonna get this chick," I was saying to myself. I headed back to my other girl's house for the fourth of July. We had beer, weed, and pills. I always been afraid of pills. We had our get-high-supply and everything was all good for the fourth; but still, my mind was on that beautiful red thing I just met at the liquor store. Had she called me right then I would have been out of there faster than you could blink. The next day, the girl from the liquor store called me and invited me over for dinner. "I hope she's gonna be dinner," I thought to myself. When I got there, I knocked on the door and was greeted by Ms. Red (that's what I'll refer to her as from here on out). She invited me in. I took a seat on the couch, and she went into the kitchen and come back with a Budweiser in her hand. I asked her if she drank Budweiser, and she told me no but said she bought a 12 pack just for me. "Oh, hell naw!

You mean to tell me I ain't got to go spend money on this woman? Man, I got to keep this one," I thought to myself. I stayed the night with her and we slept in the same bed together but did not have sex. I won't lie and say that was easy because that was one of the hardest things I had ever done. The next night I went back to her house and I told her that I couldn't sleep in the same bed with her because it was to tempting for me and that I wanted to wait until she was ready (truthfully, I wanted her right then and there). I was pleasantly surprised when she said she was ready. It was on. I was determined to make her mine after that night.

Ms. Red was now mine, all mine. But I can't say that she was good for me. You see, by this time I had started back drinking beer, and being that I was a recovering addict I knew that it was too dangerous for me to mess around with any and all type of drugs and alcohol, which is also a drug. Within two weeks of meeting Ms. Red we were sexually involved and I was now moving in with her. She was my girl. I never had to buy any beer; we always kept two 12 packs in the refrigerator: a 12 pack of Bud and a 12 pack of Bull (I liked Budweiser and she drunk that hard stuff). This environment was pushing me back into the arms of substance abuse and addiction; it was awakening a sleeping giant within me.

One day, Ms. Red took me to a car dealership and bought me a Mitsubishi B-3000 pickup truck. That car was sharp. It was white with mag wheels on it and a sound system that would make your eardrums vibrate. She had me stuck; I mean, I wasn't going anywhere. It's sad that some of us will attempt to find love and acceptance in all of the wrong places and people; If they start buying us things we'll say that's love. But that's not love! That's just stuff! But like the Bible says, "As a man thinketh in his heart so is he."

Ms. Red had me spoiled. Everything was going smooth and perfect until…the day when a couple of boys broke into our house. After that, everything went south. Do you remember me telling you about her daughter? Well, apparently this little hot thing was inviting boys over to the house while we were out working. One day, one of those little monsters decided to unlock one of the windows to the living room, and while we were at work and she (the daughter) was at school he came back and broke into our home. After discovering our home had been burglarized I was mad as hell and wanted to kill the person responsible. I felt helpless, angry and afraid. I had so many different emotions flowing through me I felt as if I was about to explode—and to think that this was my professional day job prior to this: burglarizing homes. Right then, I understood how the people that I victimized felt.

At that point in my life I was just drinking beer. I was glad I wasn't in the place where I felt that I needed to break into houses to get money just to feed an addiction. But little did I know that this little incident (the break-in) was going to cause me to spiral headfirst back into the arms of crack cocaine. It was right around the corner and I could hear her in my spirit. I wasn't out searching for it, but my mind was in deep waters and was struggling to stay afloat. You see, when smoking and drinking I didn't feel a thing, I didn't have any cares, I didn't feel any stress nor did I feel burdened by the weight of responsibility. That 'little white girl' was calling my name.

It didn't matter how far I went; I heard her call my name. I was able to win a few rounds and keep myself clean. At this point, my mind was mainly preoccupied with finding the guy(s) that broke into our home.

After the police left our house after taking our police report, Ms. Red went back into the house to look around and see what all had been stolen; at the same time, Ms. Red's daughter was outside sitting on the power box in the front yard crying profusely. I went to her and asked her what was wrong. She began to tell me about the little boys she had over at the house and how one of them unlocked a window in the house. I then told her to follow me into the house to talk to her mom. Back inside the house she began to explain to her mom everything that happened. Upset, her mom told her to go to her room.

A couple of days went by and Ms. Red was growing more and more upset with her daughter's lack of regard for the house—she didn't want to clean up around her. Her daughter's room looked a mess. The girl wouldn't even pick up her dog's poop nor wash the dishes behind herself. This infuriated Ms. Red. "First of all," Ms. Red said one day, getting on her daughter. "You walking around here and won't help clean up the house like you got a maid walking behind you cleaning up behind you! And to top it all off, you had them boys up in my house, and they came back and stole my truck!" Her daughter just stood there with an apathetic look on her face, like she couldn't care less. Angrily Ms. Red hollered, "Girl, get your butt up stairs!" The girl turned and stormed upstairs to her room. A few minutes later, Ms. Red went upstairs to address her daughter's behavior while I stayed downstairs. Next thing I know, I was hearing loud noises coming from upstairs—"Boom! Boom! Boom!" I quickly ran upstairs to see what was going on and what I saw was not what I expected to see. I thought I was going to see Ms. Red chastising her daughter; however, what I saw was the daughter beating the heck out of her own mother.

"What the?!!" I yelled. "Man, hell! Oh, hell naw! You ain't gonna be beating up my woman!" I jumped between them and separated the two, then I pushed the daughter towards the bed and her mom out of the door. The daughter then jumped up at me like she wanted to fight me. I then pushed her back onto the bed, letting her know she had better sit her behind down rather than play with me. She then screamed at her mom,

"You going to let this man put his hands on me?!! I'm your child!! How could you??!! You taking this man over me?! You choosing him over me?!!" Ms. Red just turned around, picked up the phone, and made a call to the police who arrive about 30 minutes later. Ms. Red and I then went outside to talk to the police officer and explain to him the situation. The officer then put the little girl in the back seat of his police cruiser and took her down to the juvenile detention center. Ms. Red and I were in a state of shock. We couldn't have imagined this sweet, cute little girl could turn so bad so suddenly.

"I want you to understand what's about to take place with your daughter," I said. "This is what she's going to do: she's going to use this situation for her betterment. She will flip this thing around where she will tell the counselor that she don't want to come home as long as I am here."

"No, baby. That's not gonna happen," she replied.

"I'm telling you, girl. I'm a Capricorn and she's a Capricorn and I know how we Capricorns think. She's going to use this situation and flip it around so that I am going to have to leave this house," I said. And just like I told Ms. Red, that's what happened. About two weeks later, I came home and Ms. Red was sitting at the table with this look on her face. I asked her what was wrong. She answered, "I got a call today from the counselor at the juvenile and they want to let my baby come home, but she said as long as you are here she don't want to come home." I looked at her and I knew that it was time for me to go.

"Look man, I am not going to come between you and your child. That's your baby. I understand. I'll find me somewhere to go tomorrow. I'll be alright."

"Baby, you don't have to go."

"Yes I do. If it was me and that was my baby, I love you but you got to go," I replied. Ms. Red asked me to stay until after she moved, which I did. I stayed for another week and we ended up moving out to Kennesaw, GA., then her daughter came home. When she got home I got an opportunity to talk to her. I asked her what happened and why did she change on me, and she told me that she never did agree with her mother allowing me to come and stay with them.

"I thought y'all was moving too fast," she said. "Because you met her one week and you was moving in with us the next week. She asked me what I thought and I said 'Please wait.'"

Me and Ms. Red did move fast. I'll admit that. After telling me this, I went to her mother and said, "I thought you said you spoke with her (the daughter) and asked her about me moving in here? Why you didn't tell me how she felt?" Ms. Red looked at me and said,

"I get lonely, too. I need somebody to love me. What about me? What am I supposed to do?"

I looked at her in a different light after she said that. To me then, there was something not quite right about this. "You mean to tell me you would rather choose a man over your child? You ain't no good, girl. You crazy as hell, too," I thought to myself. I left that day, but not for good. I made a couple of more trips to have sex with Ms. Red. Our relationship never did amount to anything more than that. I moved back home with my dad and stayed there for a while.

Remember when I told you that this relationship wasn't good for me? Well, I found out that going back to the alcohol put me on a slippery slope back towards the drugs—not to mention the stress of the entire household situation. I needed to cope. I needed to escape. I needed to get…high. I found myself going back to drugs. This time, I found myself smoking dope while driving a truck. I was smoking while on duty, driving up and down the street with tons of steel on the back of my truck. I was now smoking like there was no tomorrow. My addiction got so bad that I didn't care about anything and anyone; I didn't even want a girlfriend. I became antisocial but at least I had commonsense enough to quit my job before I killed someone.

CHAPTER 15:
THE BLACK WIDOW

BACK IN MY OLD NEIGHBORHOOD I MET THIS GIRL; she wasn't all that to look at. To be honest, she was messed up from the floor up. If you have never done drugs before, good; stay away from them; they will have you messing with people you wouldn't normally associate with; they'll cause you to make dumb choices, especially when high. Have you ever been in a night club when the lights are low? Everyone in the club looks good to you. You then decide to go and take a seat at the bar and start drinking, and while there you look over to your right, so drunk you can barely hold your head, and notice a woman sitting next to you. She then looks over at you and gives you one of the biggest smiles you've ever seen; and to you at that moment, she looks like the most beautiful thing in the world. The two of you start to make small talk, finding each other interesting to talk to. Everything you say is funny to her. You tell her that she's cute and fine and that you want to spend some time with her. She's cool with that. She then slides a little closer to you. You're somewhat notice that the people around you are staring at you like you've lost your cotton-picking mind. You're wondering why they're staring at you like you're crazy. You finally take her home that night and do all sorts of things to her, but when you wake up the next morning and you see what's lying next to you in your bed it is bad enough to make you get on your knees and start crying out to God—this 'thing' done scared the hebie-jeebies out of you! That's the position I found myself in. Lord have mercy! This is the type of decision that you make when you are on crack cocaine or drugs in general.

The day I met this girl I was in my truck coming home from work. I had already relapsed in my mind. Relapse is when you are doing something in your mind—you mentally see yourself doing something and it becomes so real in your mind that you actually get the sensation of doing it. I believe that's why Christ said that if a man looks at a woman and lusts in his heart after her he has already committed adultery. There I was coming home from work when suddenly I decided to go over into the neighborhood across from mine to get me a "chicken head" (a "chicken head" is a woman who is on crack cocaine so badly that she will do anything you tell her to do as long as you hook her up with some crack cocaine and/or alcohol). I went over to the next neighborhood and went to the dope man and asked him where I could find a chicken head. He said they were around there somewhere. I asked him if he had any drugs on him and he said he only had some "nickel sacks". I told him to give me two "nicks". He looked at me and was like

"For real, man?"

"Yeah" I said. "Give me two."

"Hey Steven, welcome back," he said while giving

me the drugs.

The only thing that was on my mind at this time was getting crack and finding a chicken head, although, deep down inside, I really didn't want to find a chicken head because I had every intention on smoking the crack all by myself. I bought the two bags of crack and drove off without looking for a woman. I got a beer can, put holes in it, put cigarette ashes on top of it, and started smoking the crack. I began to smoke more and more and also think of more and more ways to get money to buy more crack. Before I knew it, I quit my job, left the girl I was dealing with, and was out giving people rides to different places for a hit of crack. After a while, I stopped giving people rides because that was too slow for me. I knew a way that I could make quick money. So I started going into empty houses and taking the appliances: the refrigerators, stoves, washers and dryers, etc. I would take them to the appliance man who would buy just about anything from me. But after a while, even that got too slow for me.

One day, I recruited a guy to be my assistant in crime. We would go out and steal stoves and other appliances and then take them to the appliance guy or the corner flea market. But one particular day, I was driving down Candler Road, and I looked to my right and noticed that an appliance store was open (mind you that this was early in the morning and I needed my morning "fix"). I had my morning all planned out: I was going to steal a stove and then sell it in order to buy a 50 cent slab and a case of beer, and then find a girl. We stole a stove out of the store. While in my car, it happened so fast: "Bam!!!!" I ran into a gray SUV; it pulled out in front of me. It's funny because I had a plate of food in my lap at that time, which I was eating. After hitting the truck, I don't know what happened to that plate of food. It just vanished…like that truck ate it or something. The top part of the stove I stole was in the street. Luckily for us, the stove did not spill over the top of the truck and cause any severe damage. When the police arrived, they took down my license plate number and the other person's license plate number also our insurance information. I had insurance, but the other person didn't. The officer then gave her (the other person) a ticket and then arrested her for not having proper paperwork; he then let me go. Thank God.

After the police left, my partner and I went on to the appliance store and sold the stove for a little to nothing; we then went and got some dope, got high, and began thinking of more ways to get more money. This went on for about three months before it began to be too slow for me. I figured there had to be a better way to get dope. I wanted to be able to make one hit a day, and that meant I needed money to accomplish that goal. So, I figured I had to go back to doing what I knew how to do well: burglarize homes. That night, while laying in my bed, begin to think about neighborhoods I knew I would find money in, neighborhoods where the people were gullible and carefree and didn't lock their windows and doors and would leave their keys in their cars and doors to their homes where easily accessible.

I got up the next morning and walked around nine miles away from my neighborhood to another neighborhood, a more expensive neighborhood. While there I walked around the neighborhood searching for my victim. Again, I could feel spirits guiding me to these homes. One thing I learned is this: you better be careful who you associate with, because you will start resembling them. Like some have said before: "Association brings on simulation." And since I was associating so much with the devil and receiving instructions from him, I started to resemble him, not physically but mentally. He was leading me to places I had never been before. It was like some kind of magical force, some supernatural power that had me in its clutches. 'I never been to that house before, so how did I know to go there? How did I know to go to that door or window and it would be open? How did I know to go to that room, and that particular area in the room, which just happened to have what I was looking for? How did I know?' The Bible says in Ephesians 6:12, "For we wrestle not against flesh and blood but against principalities, against powers, against the rulers of the darkness of this world, against spiritual wickedness in high places." Spirits were leading me to those neighborhoods, to the houses and apartments, to the merchandise therein. I was getting bold with my deeds, too. I would burglarize a house and then catch the bus back home carrying the goods. One day, I got up, got dressed, went up the street and caught the bus, but I had no particular destination in mind. I just rode the bus until I saw a neighborhood that I had never been to before. When I found one, I got off of the bus and started walking up one street and down another street until I saw a house I wanted to rob. I could feel my sixth sense kicking in. I went up to the house, knocked on the front door, went around to the back of the house, looked through a window, went to the back door and, lo and behold, it was unlocked. While inside the house, I went to the bedroom closet, looked down on the floor, found a safe, got all of the contents out of it, put them in a bag, walked out of the door and told uttered the words "Thank you for your support" before getting back on the bus and going back to my neighborhood to get high all night long. This became my daily routine.

After about a year of doing this, it started to get boring to me. I wanted to find a way to make burglarizing more exciting. Perhaps, it was my addiction calling for more of a challenge; or maybe, it was the demons pushing me to go further into sin. And further into sin I was going. I was developing an addiction that went beyond crack cocaine and alcohol now: I was becoming addicted to what I thought was power. I was getting high off of the power to go into people's homes and take from them whatever I wanted; the power to strip them down to nothingness, rip their souls apart and catapult them into a place of fear; the power to dominate their thinking and alter their lives. I even developed my own trademark burglary line: I'd always say "Thank you for your support" after robbing a person's house and while leaving out of it. Jesus said in John 10:10, "...the enemy come not but for to steal and to kill and to destroy." And believe me, He was right. The enemy for me was the inner me; it had me out there destroying lives and causing people to move from the sanctuary of their homes. I'd go back into the neighborhoods I robbed and discover that the people I victimized had moved.

One house I burglarized late at night while its owners were there and fast asleep. I considered myself a cat burglar during this time because I would take my shoes off so I wouldn't make any noise while I moved around a house—you know, like a cat. A cat will enter into a room where you are and you will never know it's there unless it jumps into your lap or meows. I went into this couple's bedroom while they were asleep, got the man's wallet and the woman's purse, went back into the living room and took the money out of his wallet and their car keys out of her purse, then took the wallet and purse back into their bedroom, placed the covers over them like a mother would her child, said to them "Thank you for your support" and then walked out of the door, got into their car, and took off. I sold their car for drugs. I started doing everything I thought I was big and bad enough to do. I became what you would call an uncommon burglar—you know, the type that dressed in a suit and tie, showed up at your house in the afternoon (around 3-4 o'clock), greet you at the door, win you over and cause you to let me in your house, then sneak around while you're in the other room and steal what I could carry in my pockets that was of value, and then make off with your stuff.

Now, about that girl I told you about earlier, the one that looked a hot mess....

I remember picking up a friend of mine; we were looking for a place to smoke. She said she knew a place where we could go. So we went over to some apartments on the other side of Memorial Drive. We went into an apartment unit and everyone was smoking all over the place. She took me into a back room and there she was, lying on the bed looking like a black chocolate queen. She got up, looked at me, and smiled. I smiled back at her. I didn't notice that all of her teeth were rotten. It had never dawned on me that she was only somewhat attractive due to the makeup she had on, which was very thick—it covered all of her blemishes. The only thing that I noticed at the moment was this fine, black, beautiful woman in front of me who loved to smoke just like me. She asked me for my name and I told her. I asked her for her name and she told me. After getting that out of the way, we could finally get to business and start smoking. We smoked a lot. But crazily, every time I'd take a hit of the glass pipe, I would jump up, go to the window, and look out at my truck, thinking someone was going to try to steal it. The girl would then say, "It's okay, Steve. It's okay. Sit down. Sit down." I would then sit down and relax for a minute, hit another piece of crack, jump back up again and run to the window, looking to see if anyone was trying to steal my truck. This went on all night long and way into the next morning. As I got ready to leave, I looked back at this black woman, and for some reason, I didn't want to go; she did something that night that captured my soul. We didn't have sex; we just talked and smoked; but something happened: my mind was a little foggy by this point and I couldn't quit figure it out. It was as if I was caught up in a black widow spider's web. This woman was not attractive at all, and yet, I found myself going back to her over and over again.

CHAPTER 16:
TRAPPED

I KNEW THAT I WAS HEADING TO HELL WHILE RIDING first class. I became infamous in my neighborhood. There was no one there to stop me. I wanted to stop, but I couldn't stop myself.

I began going into more houses just to get money to buy dope so that I could be with her. We began having sex; and to tell you the truth, she wasn't all that, but I found myself going back to her like a puppet on a string. I remember one day, I had another friend of mine riding in my truck. We weren't smoking any crack, but we were drinking. I had a fifth of Crown Royal and she had a fifth of JJ. We were simply drinking, smoking weed, and talking—you know, "kicking the bo bo". She was my friend, my partner; it wasn't about sex. We didn't want to have sex. We were riding around until I decided that I wanted to get some drugs. So we went to the crack house. When I pulled up, "the black widow" came outside. When she saw me and my friend sitting in my truck, she attacked my friend. But she didn't know who she was messing with. My friend got out of the truck and chased her around the truck, shouting, "If I get my hands on you, I'm gonna beat your butt." Still chasing the woman, my friend said, "Girl, you better be glad I can't get my hands on you because I'll beat your butt out here in the yard so bad, girl! I'll drag you like a rag doll out here!" she yelled.

"Girl, what's wrong with you?! I don't go with you! You ain't my woman. And I can have whoever I want to have in my truck!" I yelled at the black widow.

"Yes, I am [your woman], and you are my man!" she responded.

It's crazy because, even after that incident, I still found myself looking for the black widow. She would not let me go. It didn't matter what I did, she was always there. I told her that she was not my girl; however, at night, when no one was looking, I kept running back to her, or I was out trying to find her.

One day, I was in the neighborhood opposite of ours just kicking it with some friends of mine when one of my friends, Dino, walked up to me and said, "You know, Black Widow is over at your house right now talking to your sister."

"What?! How you know?"

"Because I was over there looking for Ann and I saw Black Widow talking to your sister, Cat." I told Dino to get in my truck and we sped off. When I pulled up to my house there she was standing outside talking to Catherine. My brother, Joe, had a red dump truck he was working on while the Black Widow was leaning up against it. I put my foot to the pedal. I had every intention to kill her. I wanted her out of my life for good. My sister looked at me like I was crazy. I got out of the truck like a mad man. I just wanted this woman to get away from my house. Once she was gone, my sister and I had a few unkind words to say to one another; but I didn't care about that—as long as this woman was gone, I was good. I jumped back into my truck, went back to where I came from, and continued what I was doing, which was nothing. Later that night, I was at home and everyone was sleeping when I heard a knock on my window. At first, I wasn't paying it too much attention to it. I was laying on my bed looking at TV and thought that maybe it was a tree or an acorn knocking up against the window. But then, I heard another knock, and another, on the window; so I got up and looked out the window and it was the crazy woman again (Black Widow), throwing rocks at my window. I opened the window and asked her what she wanted. She said she wanted to come in. I asked her for what. She said she wanted to be with me. I told her to go away and that I didn't want to be with her, although I did deep down inside. I couldn't stand her, didn't like her, and was sick of her, but for some reason my mind was so twisted that I couldn't resist her and avoid falling weak to her ugly beauty. I got up, went downstairs and let her in; but I did it reluctantly, not happily. Perhaps, I let her in because I thought I was going to get some that night, or maybe get high. This was one of those nights I didn't do anything stupid (rob a house), so I didn't have any money to buy drugs. Satan knows how to keep you entangled in his trap. I let this woman in my house and allowed her to go upstairs to my room. We got high and had sex. Afterwards, I went downstairs and fixed her something to eat. When I went back up to my room she was asleep. I frowned because she was not my taste; actually, to be blunt, she was butt-ugly, but I was stuck. I dealt with this woman for nearly four months before finally saying enough was enough and deciding to reclaim my integrity and leave this "thing" alone.

After my decision to leave the black widow woman alone, my nephew came over to the house and brought two fine women over. One was a school teacher. She liked me even despite me being as skinny as a bean pole due to losing a lot of weight from smoking crack cocaine. I wasn't looking my best; even still, this woman still liked what she saw. I guess she saw potential in me. We were sitting in the living room talking, just having a decent conversation when, all of a sudden, there was a knock on my front door. I went to see who it was and, yes, you guessed right, it was the Black Widow. She said, "Steven, I need to talk to you." I stepped out the door to talk to her. "Who is that you got in the house?" she asked.

"Why you worried about it? That has nothing to do with you. That is none of your concern."

"But you are my man."

"The hell if I'm your man! I'm not your man! What do you want?!"

"Who is that?!"

"Friends! What do you want?!"

"Oh, so you got those whores in your house and I'm pregnant with your baby!" I was looking at this woman like she lost her mind.

"Girl, get out of my face with that garbage you are talking about! Go on about your business! I ain't got time for these games! Go about your business, now!"

I turned to go back into the house when she

rushed up to me. I turned around and said, "Look now, I done told you once, I'm not gone say it again: Go on about your business leave me alone. I am not your man. You are not my woman. Go away. Leave me alone. It's over. I'm done. Leave me the hell alone." She then went out into the street in front of my house and started pacing back-and-forth, talking about she's going to call the police.

"You done got me pregnant, Stephen! You done got me pregnant and you got those whores up in your house, and I got your baby inside of me! I'm going to call the police on you because you my man!" she yelled.

She was saying all type of crazy stuff. I can't remember everything that she said, but it was crazy. While she was outside shouting and yelling crazy stuff, I was inside of the house listening.

"Who was that?" the school teacher asked.

"I don't know," I responded.

"Yeah, you do know what that is."

"Hold up. Wait a minute," I said to her. I then got up and went outside to confront the black widow woman. "If you don't get the hell away from my house I'm going to call the police on you! Now leave me alone! You are not my woman! You are not my woman! Get this through your thick skull! You are not my woman!" I yelled. She then walked away. After that, I went back into the house to finish spending time with the school teacher; however, the black widow woman did her job: she prevented me from getting with this woman.Even though she was determined not to see me happy with another woman, I refused to go back to her. I was done. I was just glad to no longer be entangled in her deadly web. I was glad I had my mind back…at least from her.

I began venturing out into other neighborhoods at night. I eventually lost my truck due to drugs; and as a result thereof, I now had to walk around and commit my burglaries at night. At first, I would do the burglaries, get the money, then go home with a lot of dope, which I would smoke by myself, but that got boring again. I felt the need to find somebody to smoke with, which I did. I found multiple people. I would avoid home as much as possible because it was too quiet there for me. My father was a preacher and I didn't want to disrespect him. At least, that was one of the excuses that I'd use. Another excuse I use was that I didn't want to steal from him. But the truth was I just wanted to be independent and smoke as much dope and do as much damage as I possibly could without being bothered. I did not want to be limited. I wanted the freedom to do whatever I wanted to do whenever I wanted to do it, how I wanted to do it.

One night, I went to break in a house in Decatur. When I got to the house, this lady, her husband, and their children were home. I looked for her purse so I could take the keys to their truck and so I could put all my stolen goods in the truck. I remember going to the bedroom door to open it. Now, this was not your typical bedroom door; this door did not open like your normal door; you had to slide it to open and close it. While attempting to open the door, I had awakened the lady. She said, "Who is that?" At that point she saw me. I then ran towards the back door while she was in hot pursuit after me. Even while running, I still had the audacity to reach for her purse. "Who are you?!" she yelled.

"Tony, the Tiger," I yelled back while running out

of the door as fast as I could. Realizing I wasn't going to outrun the police, I ran to the house next door and hid in some bushes. When the police arrived, I heard them talking to her.

"He ran that way," I overheard her telling them. When they got back in their car to look for me, I got up ran in the other direction. I ran behind houses, through back yards, tripping and falling over things, and even flipped over a fence, hurting myself in the process. I knew that if they caught me I was going back to prison, which I was determined not to let happen. While running and hiding it dawned on me that I was running in the wrong direction.

"Man, I got to go back the way I came," I remember saying to myself. So I turned around and began heading the other way, heading home. While running home, my legs were throbbing with pain—they were were cut up and bleeding from the branches and brambles from the bushes and trees. When the police would go down one street, I would go up the other street, running from house to house and crossing over from side to side. One house I hid behind had a backyard full of kudzu—it was summertime. I dove into the kudzu bush to hide from the police, but it appeared to be filled with snakes. I swore I saw something moving in those bushes to my right. Imagined or not, I got the hell up out of there. Drugs will make you do the craziest things. I went to the other side and found myself in familiar area: I was now in the Samuel L. Jones, Eastlake Community. While doing all of that running back and forth, I still held on to this woman's purse. I held on to it as if it were my life support. I reached a house I could hide in, and began going through the poor lady's purse, searching for money and her identity. You see, by this time I had become very familiar with identity fraud, too; I knew how to get a credit card and get money from a victim. I was rambling through her purse, but there were no credit cards; the only thing that I found of value was five dollars. I risked my life and my freedom over five stinking dollars? Yes! I could have gone back to prison that night over five stinking dollars I thought to myself as I headed back towards my neighborhood.

Not too long afterwards, I moved into a rooming house where there was a girl I was dealing with. I remember the two of us being in the room one night—we had no electricity, just candles burning in the room and a battery powered radio playing. The girl was sitting on the other side of the bed. I loved taking pictures; so, every time I would break into a house I would steal the person's camera—digital camera, 8 mm camera; it did not matter. On this night, I had a digital camera. I was taking pictures of the girl when something caught my attention; it was coming from the left side of the room where the music was playing. I turn my head and saw this thing floating across the room. It was about 3 feet tall and 4 feet wide, and it was shaped like a rectangle; it was transparent. It reminded me of the movie "Predator" staring Arnold Swcharsnegger, when the monster was cloaked in stealth mode. You could vaguely see it or sense it, but barely; however, you knew it was there. This thing floated across the room from my left and was heading towards my girl. Shocked, just watched it. By the time it got to my girl, I came to my senses, lifted my camera, and snapped a picture of it. When I looked at the picture, all I saw was a cloud of smoke; it was like a fog came over the lens of the camera and hovered over her. The picture was very unclear; it was very misty; but when we looked at the rest of the pictures, they were very clear. I could see this thing just as clearly as I can my own hand. While just staring at the camera, my girl looked at me and asked,

"What's wrong?" I didn't respond. I just sat there silently. "Baby, what's wrong?" she asked again. Finally, I broke my silence.

"Baby, you got to come see this!" I said. She got up, walked around the bed, and came to my side. "Baby, look." She looked at the picture and tried to process what she was seeing.

"Man, that's just cigarette smoke," she claimed.

"Baby, we ain't smoking," I responded. I then told her what I saw before I took the picture.

"Well, I'm about to go back to my room," she said unfazed—at the time, she was living in one of the other bedrooms at that rooming house. After she left, hung around my room for another 20 minutes cleaning up, and then went to her room to spend the night there.

The next morning, I got dressed and left the house, going on one of my adventures. After going out and doing what I did best, I returned to my room. I hit a big lick (that's what we call obtaining something of great value while stealing) that brought me quite a deal of money. Now, I had plenty of dope, plenty to drink, and all the cigarettes I wanted, and I was having a good time. I had so much dope I decided I to sell some. That night, I stayed up selling and smoking dope and drinking. Afterwards, I went home, locked down my room, and went to bed. The next morning, when I woke up, I looked under my bed to get a morning blast ("a wake up" as we called it, which is another term for smoking dope in the morning), all my dope and money was gone. Everything I had worked so hard for the day before was gone. I figured a crack head had come into my room while I was asleep and stole everything. Boy, I was mad! I stormed out my room, yelling at the top of my lungs, "Who been in my room?!!!" Everyone just stared at me like I lost my mind. "I know one of y'all been in my room because my dope is gone and my money is gone!! Who been in my room??!! I'm going to kick somebody's butt around here if it's the last thing I do! I can't have nothing around here! Every time I try to do something, y'all want to come in here and mess me up! I'm sick of y'all!"

I figured at that point that I had no choice but to go and do another burglary. I was starting to grow tired of jeopardizing my freedom, but my addiction had me trapped. I went back to my room, laid down, and went back to sleep. After waking up again, I decided to go to the bathroom and freshen up before leaving the house. I went into the bathroom, stood in front of the mirror, turned the water on, and started to wash my face and brush my teeth—although a junkie, I still took care my hygienic needs. I remember picking up the rag and soaking it in water. When I got ready to apply it to my face, I happened to catch a quick glance of myself in the mirror. I looked into my eyes and was frightened by what I saw. I immediately turned my head away and looked down. What I saw scared me. I saw an evil in my eyes, in my soul. I saw a hatred that was monstrous living inside of me. What was in me whispered in my soul, "I want to kill you. You are going to die." I was too afraid to look back at my reflection in the mirror at that point. After that, I stopped looking into my own eyes. I got worse. My addiction grew worse. I started doing things more boldly. I did not care who saw me. I dared the police to come after me. In the upcoming days I found myself in high-speed car chases, going into homes at night more and more, smoking more dope than ever, and being completely out of control. I knew that I was heading to hell while riding first class. I became infamous in my neighborhood. There was no one there to stop me. I wanted to stop, but I couldn't stop myself.

CHAPTER 17:
OUT OF CONTROL

My last night on the street is one that I will never forget. I just did a major burglary and ended up with so much dope and money that it was ridiculous. I went up Glenwood, got a hotel room, and got three women. We were doing all kinds of things in that room, things I dare not mention in this book. When done with them, one of them decided that she wanted to stay with me. Her idea was to go out and sell herself and come back and bring me the money. "If that's what you want to do, fine. Go ahead. I'm not going to stop you, but I'm not making you do it either," I told her. She went out, sold her body, came back, gave me the money, went back out again, sold her body, came back, brought me the money; but on the third time, she went out and then came back with a "John" (guy who solicits sex from prostitutes). She then asked if I would leave the room so that she could have sex with the guy. I looked at her like she had lost her mind and said, "No. If you want to have sex, here's the bed. Go at it." They began to have sex right in front of me while I was looking at TV.

They were laying beside me having sex. I looked at him and said, "It's good, ain't it, man?" Then I looked back at the television. When they got through, he gave her the money, and she then handed it to me. But the guy did not want to leave, so I had to make him leave.

A few days later, a friend of mine came to the hotel room with a female friend of his. When she saw me, she smiled and said, "Ooooh, who is this handsome guy?" I didn't answer her. She looked at me and asked if I had a girlfriend. I told her no. Then she said she was going to take me home with her. "That's fine by me," I thought. I did not have any more money anyway, and that was the last day that I had in that room. So I went to her house and basically moved in that day. That night we had sex. I woke up the next morning to the smell of pancakes and sausages. She brought me breakfast in bed. I felt like a King. She had a car that she would not allow anyone to drive, but by the end of the week I had the keys to it and was driving it. While she was asleep in the bed, I would go out and do burglaries in her car. During one particular job, I got a lot of money; however, I was tired of smoking, tired of drinking, tired of the life that I was living. I began to realize that life did not do this to me; I chose this type of life. But now I was tired of getting high. One this particular night, after getting high, I went to sleep and had a dream. In my dream, I was running from the police; and no matter how fast I ran, I wasn't fast enough. It was strange because I had run away from the police plenty of times before and had even been in high-speed car chases and have escaped, so why couldn't I get away from the police this time in my dream? When I woke up, I told my girl about the dream. The interesting thing is whenever I would dream about the police or going to prison or being in those type of situations, I would usually end up there. I would occasionally experience déjà vu, where I saw myself going to jail or to prison. I believe déjà vu is God trying to show you where you're headed. He would show me where I was going before I got there. All I needed to do was pay attention and listen closely to Him. I dreamt that I was being chased by a police officer and he caught me. After having that dream, I went on about my business like nothing happened. About two days later, I did another burglary, but this time, I made up in my mind that I was not going to continue burglarizing people; I was going to take the money, buy some dope, and sell it; I was going to flip the money instead.

I went into my old neighborhood to get some dope from one of the guys I used to deal with, but when I got to his house the police pulled up and started calling everyone. I started walking and didn't look back. I was mimicking Lot, who the angel of the Lord told to leave Sodom and Gomorrah and to not look back. The officer stopped everyone except for me. I went across Candler Road with my drugs in hand, and ran back towards my neighborhood. I took a left, ran down Morgan Place, made another left and was running back up Salmon Hill. I got back to Candler Road, made my way across the street, and went back towards the house (I had to go back because I used my girl's car and I was not going to leave it there). When I got back, I saw the dope dealer walking down the street. I asked him where the police was and he said they were gone. I then got in my girl's car and pulled off, but I forgot that I had an old friend riding with me that night. I saw him talking to a girl, the same girl that introduced me to the black widow woman. I told him to get in the car, then we took off. When I got back to the area where I was kicking it at, I began to sell what I bought. I sold out very quickly. I then called my guy and told him that I needed another quarter ounce of crack, which he agreed to supply. We were to make our rendezvous on Memorial Drive; one of our destinations was a Shell gas station located on the corner of Rockbridge and Memorial Drive, just down the street from the Dekalb County jail. I went out to meet my supplier, got in the car, and I headed in his direction. It's amazing how your life can change in a blink of an eye. I got to Memorial Drive and made a right turn at the red light, not seeing the sign that said "No turn on red". Right while I was turning, a police car was coming up the street in my direction. When they saw me making that illegal turn, they cut on their lights and got behind me, pulling me over. I was use to being chased by the cops, but by now I was tired of doing so. I pulled over. The officer got behind me, stepped out of his car, came to my window, and asked me for my information. I told him I didn't have my wallet and then gave him the wrong information. He went back to process the name I gave him. A few seconds later, he came back and asked me for my social security number. I told him I did not know my social security number. He then said, "You mean to tell me you're a grown man and you don't know your social security number? Man, get out of the car." I got out of the car and he searched me; he then put me in the back of his police cruiser and ran my information. That's when the truth came out. He discovered that I was Stephen O'Neal

Howard. He then said, "Yeah, Mr. Howard, we got you."
At that point, I began to plead like a babe,

"Please let me go! Please let me go! You don't
know what Cobb County gonna do to me, man! They
gave me 20 years, and if I go back I'm gonna do all of it.
Please let me go!" But the police officer wasn't trying to
hear any of it. I continued to plead: "I'm never coming
home! Please let me go! Don't do this! Please let me go!"
I was angry because I let this guy lock me up. When I
finally calmed down, I asked him if I could call my friend
so that she could come and get her truck. He said yes. I
called my friend and she came around the corner and got
the keys to her truck. I had some money in my pocket,
and instead of taking it to jail with me, I gave her some of
it and then I went on to jail that night. That was the last
time that I saw her or anyone else in that neighborhood
again. I knew that I was going away for a long time this
time.

I went to the County jail that night. By 8 o'clock
that morning, the Cobb County Sheriff was there to pick
me up. Before 12 o'clock noon, I was in a Cobb County
Jail. I sat in that Cobb County jail for about a week before I went in front of a Judge. But this time, I had a very
bad experience. It had been a long time since I shaved
my face and my head. I was looking like a zombie—like
The Walking Dead to a degree. When I reached Cobb
County, in my dorm I was given a razor—the officers
gave everyone the opportunity to shave. I realized that I
had to appear in front of a Judge, and that it wasn't wise
to stand before the judge with a face full of hair. I got my
razor and took a shower. It had been a long time since I
saw a shower. Even when I was staying with the last girl,

I did not take a shower; I used to wash under my arms and between my legs—you know, take one of those bird baths. This time, I got in the shower and cleaned myself up. When I came out of the shower, I stood before the mirror and, for the first time in months, I looked at myself. I looked in my eyes and still felt a deep sense of menace and hatred, but this time I was not afraid. I began to shave my face and my head. Oh my God, it felt so gooooood! After that, I went to bed, but when I woke up the next morning, the right side of my face appeared as if I had been stung by 100 bees. My face was so swollen. It scared the dickens out of me. I went to the buzzer to call the officer, but he paid me no attention. I started beating on the door in order to get his attention. When he finally came to the speaker, he asked, "What is your problem?" "Look!!!" I said, pointing at my face. He came around, got me, and rushed me down to the nurse. When the doctor saw me, he said I had staph in my face. "What?!"

"You have a staph infection in your face and we have to do surgery immediately," he responded. I didn't know what to think. I had never experienced anything like that before. I figured my face was going to be disfigured and I was going to look like a monster for the rest of my life. I had all kinds of crazy thoughts and pictures going through my head. "I am disfigured for the rest of my life. No one is going to like me now. They're not going to even glance my way, except to talk about me," I thought to myself.

All my life I thought of myself as a pretty boy; but now, I got myself in a messy situation—my face was messed up. The doctor performed certain procedures on my face: he cut the right side of my face open towards my ear and removed all of the poison, and then packed the wound with gall. He said they had to leave the wound open so they could clean it every day. The next day, I went back down to the nurse's station to get the wound cleaned; that was a pain that I care not to experience again. We assumed that my face was healing properly until one morning I woke up and, again, my face began to swell. I went back down to the nurse's station and the doctor came out, examined my face, then said the staph infection had spread; he then told me he had never seen this happen in a long time and that I had what they called an aggressive staph. Once again, he had to cut into my face, remove the infection, pack it with gall, and send me back to my dorm. I just knew then that I was completely disfigured in my face. A couple of days later I had to stand before the Judge. I'll never forget her it. The judge seemed so happy to send me back to prison, although I couldn't blame her. She had given me a chance before and I messed it up. I violated my parole, which meant I had to go back to prison to complete my time. I just had to deal with it; that was my attitude. But, in a way, I felt relieved because I was free from drugs. I figured that, maybe, when I got out the next time, I would stay free from drugs and alcohol; that there was a chance. I started to add up the years that I had to do and said to myself, "Well, you won't be that old when you get out. You'll still have a little life left in you."

I went back to my dorm and excepted my fate. I remember sitting on my bunk—there was this Hispanic guy sitting on his bunk next to me. I didn't say too much to him at first, and vice versa. But I noticed that everyday he would go to the table and all of the Hispanics would crowd around the table, and he would talk to them. I never saw a Bible, but I knew that he was conducting a Bible study. One day, while sitting on our bunks, I asked him if I could ask a question. He said yes. I asked him, "When you are at the table and everyone is around you, are you doing Bible study?"

"Yes," he responded. From that day on, we began to talk. We talked about life. I remember asking him what was the story behind his arrest. After he shared with me his story, he asked me mine. I felt sorry for him because he was just a victim who got caught up in a bad situation. I began to tell him about God. I began to tell him as much as I knew about the Bible; after all, I was raised in church and I knew the Word of God, although I did not live it. I began to share with him the Word, and he would in turn take what I shared with him back to his brothers at the table. One day, I was teaching him the Word, and when I got finished, it was time for them to have their Bible study. He then got up and went to the table. I then leaned back on my bed to relax. At that point, I heard the voice of God, saying,

"I am giving you an international ministry."

"What?!! Whatever!!" I remember responding. After that, I didn't think too much else about it. But I began to pick up my Bible and read it. You see, God will use people in the strangest places to help you along the way. While I was teaching this young man the Word of God, his life was teaching me the Word of God.

Chapter 18:
PLAYING MYSELF

I was lying on my bunk when the announcement was made. I jumped off of my bunk, put my shoes on, and ran to the door. Once the door opened, I was one of the first ones to run out to the yard. Everyone was rushing to the yard; they were rushing to get the basketballs, and the baseballs and baseball gloves; they were rushing to get to the workout area and the bingo area; everyone had their own agenda, and I had mine. My agenda was to rob the children of God. But God had other plans.

GOD WANTED TO PUT ME IN A SITUATION AND position where I had no other choice but to humble myself so that I could hear Him, and it didn't matter that by nature I was stubborn, hardheaded, bullheaded, and selfish. God spoke into my spirit, "I want you to humble yourself. I need you to be quiet so that you can hear Me when I speak to you." I began to read my Bible more often. I soon found myself forming a Bible study for those who spoke English. You see, even before I went back to prison, I had already started going back to church. Something inside of me was changing. When I got back to prison, they had a piano there. I wanted to play the piano. I approached the preacher who would come on Sundays to minister to us and asked him if he would allow me to play the piano. He responded,

"Please, yes."

While I played the piano, he was moved and touched. He then approached me and asked, "Brother, when are you getting out?"

"I don't know," I said. "I got a long time."

"When you get out, come and find me. I need someone that can play the piano like you do."

God was truly dealing with me at this time, but I wasn't completely paying attention to Him. I was still in selfish mode, doing a lot of stuff just to kill time. I had not fully settled on the idea of giving my life to Christ. Sell out to the Lord? For what? I'm in jail! I'm going to prison! This is my life! Who can I help?! That was my thinking. So I never gave the preacher's offer any real thought.

I slipped into a daily routine: lay around all day or go to the tables which we used as our dining room and make up games—they did not allow us to have card games, board games, or any other similar games. Even still, we would recreate these games. But the officers would always come by and confiscate them. Mostly, everyone just walked around the dorm like zombies or sat on bunks reminiscing over the past. As time continued, the days seemed to get shorter. I knew it was about time for me to be shipped back to prison. I remember that morning: it was around 1 o'clock and everyone that had been sentenced to prison was in great expectation. We just wanted to get away from jail, which was truly a hell hole no one wanted spend their time in. It was better to be in a prison than in a jail. In prison, there is more freedom. In prison, I could play my games; in jail, I couldn't. In prison, I could go to the store; in jail, I couldn't. In prison, I could write my love ones; in jail, I couldn't. In prison, I could walk around the yard; in jail, I couldn't. So, everyone was in great expectation when the doors finally opened that Tuesday morning. I heard an officer call my name:

"Steven Howard."

"Yes," I said, looking up.

"Pack it up. You are being shipped." Oh, the joy that came over my soul when I heard those words.

How is it that I could have such joy in my spirit while going to a place of bondage, a place of confinement, a place of separation, a place of loneliness, a place where there is no love, only hatred? I had accepted my fate. I was going to a place that was going to separate me from the world and life as I knew it. I was at peace with it. I packed my clothes, rolled up my mat, ran to the door, and was pacing back and forth while waiting on the transferring officer to come and open the door and get out of that dorm. I couldn't wait to run downstairs, change into my new clothes, and get ready to go to my new home. Sounds sad. I know. It is sad to equip and prepare yourself mentally to be comfortable in an uncomfortable place or position. But that's the position I found myself in. I knew the life of a prisoner because I had spent the last 10 years of my life in prison; so, I was ready for what prison was about to throw my way...or, at least, I thought I was ready. You see, I had a friend that was hanging on to my every word—she loved herself some Stephen. I sold her wet dreams and caviar dinners but had no intentions of fulfilling them. But, as long as I had her in my corner, I figured I was going to be okay.

When we got on the bus and began the journey down that long, lonely road, I just knew I was going back to Jackson State Prison, although my hope was that I would be going to Coaster State Prison; but lo and behold, my hoped was fulfilled because we were heading to Coaster. When I arrived, I was familiar with the running of the prison system. I quickly adapted to the operations and began hanging out in the law library, figuring that I had been cheated somehow by the court system.

I somehow thought the system had done me wrong and I was determined to find a way to get out of prison. I only needed to look up my crime and find a hole in the system I could use to get back in the face of a judge. I had it all figured out. But little did I know I was simply wasting my time because God's plan was in motion. And regardless of what I did, I could not alter His plan.

I stayed in Coaster for two months. During this time, I grew attracted to one of the nurses there. She was a bright skinned lady with pretty brown eyes and a few freckles on her face. I also became friends with an older guy. I told him about that nurse, and he said, "Man, you just got to go for what you know." So, I decided to play Mr. Debonair, Mr. Playboy, and write this woman a letter; however, in order to get the message out of the message, she had to read between the lines. I wrote this letter and I sent it to her. Evidently, she read between the lines because I got a call one day to come to the library; and when I entered the library, no one was there…except for five huge guys who were on a special forces team at the prison (the CERT Team). When I saw those guys with those huge, muscle bound arms, which looked as big as my body, standing in the library, waiting for me, I knew I was in trouble. I gathered up my courage and entered into the library anyway. At that point, one of those guys looked at me and called my name:

"Howard?"

"Yes, sir," I said.

"Do you recognize this letter?"

"Yes, sir."

"Would you mind explaining this letter to me?" the officer asked.

"Sure, sir." I began to explain the letter to the officers in a way as not to reveal its true meaning. When I finished talking, the officer looked at me and said,

"Well, that is my fiancée, and if she need protection she has me."

"Yes, sir. I'm sorry, sir. I was only trying to help, sir." The officer then looked at me and said,

"Okay, Mr. Howard. She'll be alright. Go on back to your cell." I then turned around and began walking away, and with every step that I took away from him my heart began to beat faster. I got back to my dorm and went up to my friend and told him what had just transpired and he just laughed. I couldn't help but laugh too. That was the end of that. From that moment on, every time I saw that nurse, I looked the other way. Like Kenny Rogers used to sing: "You've got to know when to hold 'em, know when to fold 'em, know when to walk away, and know when to run. You never count your money, when you're sittin' at the table. There'll be time enough for counting when the dealin's done."

I knew that this was not the time to hold them. Not too long after that I was shipped to Dodge State Prison. This was one of the worse prisons in the state of Georgia; it was a high maximum prison. I truly can't say that I know why I got shipped to this prison, considering the fact that my crime wasn't all that bad. I wondered to myself why they shipped me there? Why not just send me to a county camp like everyone else I thought. I did not see God's hand, nor did I understand His plan for me then. I quickly adapted to my environment by becoming one of the fellas. I blended in very nicely. But I still had to get myself adjusted to the way in which the Dodge State Prison was run. I did not understand why we had to get up at four in the morning just to stand outside the dorm just to be counted, and neither did I understand why I had to get back up at five just to clean my room, especially when considering that they were doing inspections around 10 am. But after a period of time, I settled in and became accustomed to the way the facility was run.

I made another friend at the prison; I'll never forget his name: it was James Fields. James was an older gentleman who was very smart and very intelligent. We would sit and play dominos all day. James would literally beat my butt in Dominos from sun-up to sundown. We did not play the regular six bones; we played nine and 12 bones Dominos. We would play 10 games a day—I might win one. Talking to James gave me a lot of wisdom concerning life in general. He shared with me things that I probably wouldn't have ever learned anywhere else even to this day. He opened my eyes and caused me to see life on an entirely different level. He gave me a deeper perspective of life. God was moving and I wasn't even unaware of it. I used to love to go to the library to get books to read. The thicker the book, the better. I remember going to the library one day and picking up a book that was very identical to the Bible; it contained 1,800 pages. While reading the book while lying on my bunk, I pulled the book down to my chest and I told myself once I got through reading that book I was going to pick up my Bible; and after making that promise, I commenced to reading that book.

One particular day, I was lying on my bunk, reading when James came to my room, opened the door, and called my name: "S.O.?" I looked up.

"Yeah," I said.

"The Christians have a Bible study on the yard every Saturday, and if you don't have any food they would give you soups and stamps for the weekend."

Allow me to explain to you why he came into my room to tell me this. Remember when I told you about a particular girl that I had wrapped around my finger around the time that I was arrested? Well, I decided to let her go because I decided that I was not going back to her once I got out. When I told her about my plans, all of my financial support ceased. God had a plan and I was right in the midst of it. Since she left, I had no money. I could not go to the store anymore. I was broke as a joke on a floating boat going nowhere fast. So, he told me about the Christians that had a Bible study every Saturday, to which I decided I needed to go so that I could get some soup and stamps from them. I wanted to use these items to buy cigarettes and coffee with. Like I said earlier, soup

175

and stamps was money in prison; you could just about get anything you wanted in prison if you had enough soups and stamps to buy it with.

Saturday morning arrived and I was anticipating a good fortune that day. I could not wait until they announced yard call. I was not one of those inmates that always went out on the yard on weekends. I usually stayed inside and read books, played Dominos, smoked cigarettes, and watch sports on television. But this Saturday was going to be a different. I was going to play those Christians like the strings on a guitar. This was going to be like taking candy from a baby. But little did I know God had a plan and I was right in the middle of it.

I was lying on my bunk when the announcement was made. I jumped off of my bunk, put my shoes on, and ran to the door. Once the door opened, I was one of the first ones to run out to the yard. Everyone was rushing to the yard; they were rushing to get the basketballs, and the baseballs and baseball gloves; they were rushing to get to the workout area and the bingo area; everyone had their own agenda, and I had mine. My agenda was to rob the children of God. But God had other plans.

CHAPTER 19:
GOD TRICKED ME

MY AGENDA WAS TO TAKE THESE CHRISTIANS' meekness for weakness and capitalize on the love of God and kindness in their hearts. I was simply selfish. When I ran out to the yard, I looked to my left and to my right, trying to find a crowd of people gathered in a circle somewhere, anything to indicate that there was a Bible study nearby. I finally spotted a crowd sitting on the bleachers. I headed straight for them. When I got to them, everyone was smiling and talking. Like a snake, I slid in and took a seat, then one of the brothers came to me and he introduced himself. I introduced myself. He said, "Welcome, brother."

"Thank you." Bible study began after that. To tell you the truth, I cannot tell you what was said at during the Bible study. I wasn't there for the Word. I had something else in mind. It was hot outside that day. The sun was beaming down on our heads. Gnats and mosquitoes were flying around and I was getting restless. "Man, I wish y'all would hurry up," I thought to myself. After what seemed like an eternity, it was now time to dismiss.

We all came down from the bleachers and formed a circle. I remember the leader of the Bible study making the announcement about the soups and stamps. He said,

"We know that there is some of you who are not able to go to the store, who are not as fortunate as some of us; so, what we decided to do was buy a little extra for those of you who are not able to go to the store. If you are one of the unfortunate ones, please step into the middle of the circle." I threw all of my pride aside and stepped in the midst of them. Again, I was just excited because I knew that I was going to get some soup and stamps. I was tired of begging and bombing cigarettes and stamps and coffee and soups, and wanted my own. But I had that same mentality when I was in the streets: I had a manipulating spirit. I was now in the middle of that circle. The leader of the Bible study called to one of the other brothers and asked, "You got the bag?"

"Yes, sir, brother," the man replied. He then pulled out a bag that was full of soups. It was about three of us in the middle of the circle at that time on that hot Saturday morning. He then handed each one of us two soups. After each one of us got our first round of soups, he came back again and gave us one more soup for a total of three a piece. Oh, man, my stomach was bubbling like I just hit the jackpot. That was the same feeling I'd get in the pit of my stomach whenever I did a burglary and knew I was about to get high. The manipulative monster had awaken again. After getting those soups, I headed back to my cell house and then bee lined straight to the store man; I then knocked on his cell door and asked,

"Hey, man, you got any cigarettes and coffee?"

"Yeah, come on in," he responded. I walked in and

he pulled out a big bag of cigarettes which had bundles of cigarettes rolled together. It was my choice which bundle I wanted. I chose the biggest bomb I saw and then he pulled out another bag that contained coffee in a finger. After getting my cigarettes and my coffee, I felt content. I went back out and found my friend James, gave him a cigarette and half of the bomb of coffee, and we sat at the table and played Dominos, drank our coffee, and smoked our cigarettes, but all the while I was thinking about how could I get some more stuff from those Christians before next Saturday. I was hatching a plan. But no sooner than I could come up with a plan, I heard a voice say in my ear,

"Go to church. The Christians are at church. You can catch them at church, and you can get anything you want from them at church." Yes! That was it! I made up in my mind at that very moment that I was going to church the next day. So I smoked the rest of my cigarettes that day, leaving only one that was for the morning—that cigarette was what we called our "morning wake up" just like any other drug.

I went on to bed that night scheming and plotting just like I use to while out in the streets, only this time, I wasn't thinking about drugs; I was, instead, thinking about more soups and stamps; this time, I wasn't thinking about what neighborhood to rob; I was thinking about robbing Christians who visited with supplies. I figured they were gullible. I crafted the perfect lie to tell them. The only thing that I had to do now was find a familiar face. When the next morning came, I got up, went to the chow hall and ate what they served every Sunday (pancakes, bananas, bologna, and coffee); and after chow, I went back to my dorm and waited for them to call for the morning worship service. At Dodge State Prison, they had an early morning worship service and also an evening service. I figured I had to catch the early morning worship service since I had no more cigarettes and therefore needed them now.

We were looking at television when suddenly the announcement came over the intercom: "Church Call! Church Call!" My stomach began to bubble. I didn't have a Bible, so I went on to church empty-handed. While I was entering the church I noticed something unusual about all the men who were going to the fellowship that morning: many of them looked happy; they had a peace about them that was obvious. Still, I just had one goal which was to get my hands on some prison money. When I got to the building I entered the room and noticed that everyone was greeting one another with a smile; they were laughing as if they had not seen one another in weeks. I found myself a seat in a corner and just observed everyone that entered into the building. I finally spotted one of the men that was in the circle the day before—a familiar face. I did not approach him as soon as he came in; instead, I decided to wait until after the service had ended. When the service began the praise team got up and started to sing; the words to the songs were being displayed on the monitors behind them as the sung. They sung about three songs before the chaplain walked in; he had some awards in his hands. After he introduced himself and welcomed everyone to the Sunday morning worship service, he said, "We have some awards for some brothers who have completed the discipleship program, and we also have Bibles for them."

He began to call their names; and when they came up to the podium, they received their reward certificate of completion and a Life Way Bible. The Bible got my attention; it was beautiful. At the time, I did not have a Bible. I quickly turned my attention back to my chaplain. I was determined not to get sidetracked from my mission. After the chaplain presented the certificate and the Bibles, he told us to turn our Bibles to the book of Matthew where he spoke on love and patience. (It's amazing how I remember that!)

After the sermon was over, I made my way over to my victim: "Hey, brother," I said.

"Hey, how you doing, brother? Is everything okay?" he asked.

"Yeah, I'm okay except…I don't know, maybe you can help me."

"Sure, what is it?"

"I've been trying to write home, but I don't have any stamps to be able to send my letters out and I need to get in contact with my family bad. I hate begging for anything, but I don't know what else to do."

"Let me see," he said. He then reached into his back pocket and pulled out his wallet. "Awe man, I don't have but one stamp. Will that help?"

"Yeah man, that would be great. I'll just send this to my mom," I replied. Of course, I was lying. He then handed me the stamp and told me if I returned to the evening service he might be able to get more stamps for me. I then pretended to be thankful and grateful towards him while really thinking of him as a sucker. Once we parted ways, I uttered those old familiar words to myself I use to say to all of my victims in the streets: "Thank you for your support."

    I went back to the dorm and bought another bomb of cigarettes with that stamp. I started preying on the Christians like a predator...or so I thought. I thought I was the one setting them up, not realizing God was setting me up. In His great wisdom, He was able to use my own weakness to bless and save me with. You see, while going to church every Sunday morning and Sunday evening, something inside of me was beginning to change. While in church one Sunday morning, the chaplain was giving out certificates of completion and Life Way Bibles, and while sitting there, I remember saying to myself, "I would love to have one of those Bibles." I wanted to hear my name get called, too, just like the other graduates in the program. I wanted to stand in front of everyone and receive my reward, too. God was working even while my flesh was working. Sure, I was only thinking about receiving recognition, but God was still using that whole situation to draw me closer to Him. After service was over that particular Sunday morning, I got a stamp from one of the brothers and then headed to the chaplain aide and asked, "Hey, so tell me how can I get one of those Bibles?"

    "You have to complete the discipleship program," he responded.

    "What is that?" I asked.

    "Wait a minute. Let me find the paperwork for you," he responded. He began to go through the folders. He then came out with a form that I had to fill out. "Here, fill this out" he said. I took the form from him, walked to the other side of the room, sat down, and began filling it out. Once I completed the form, I returned it to the aide. He reached into another folder and pulled out my schedule. "This is the schedule that you have to keep," he said. "You must read three books a week and write an essay on one of them. After writing your essay, you must return it by the end of the week to be scored. You got to pray every day. Pick you out a time of the day and pray. Every time you pray, you must keep a record on the time you prayed. You got to read two books a week out of the Bible. You must keep a record on which book you read and what was the story about and what did the Lord say to you as you read the Bible."

At first it seemed like this was an impossible task to complete. "Man, I don't know if I want to do all of this," I said to myself. "This is too much work. I want a Bible, but not that bad." I was torn in between studying, praying, reading, and writing essays, but the reward would be great in the end; my name would be called and I would receive my Bible and my certificate. So, I decided to take on the challenge. I thought to myself, "What the heck. What do I have to lose?" I went to the chaplain's library the following Friday, picked out two books that were on the list and a third book pertaining to Christianity. I went back to my dorm and started reading the books. Suddenly, I found myself becoming more engrossed in them. They were actually good. After reading the first book, I sat down at my desk and I completed my first essay, then I jumped into the next book. I started getting excited about these books because they were actually that good. After completing the second book, I picked up the third book and I began to read it. I was now learning so much about Christianity and God, more than I had ever known. After completing the first three books and reading the Bible (Oh, by the way, I decided to read the book of Matthew and Psalms), I went to church that Sunday morning and I turned in my essays at the end of the service. I received a passing score. I was excited now. I couldn't wait for Friday to get here. It couldn't come fast enough. Finally, on Friday, I rushed to the chaplain's library and pulled out three more books to read. I was also becoming familiar with the brothers at the church. The following weekend, I was one of the first to go out to the yard. I still had a smoking problem, I still used profanity, and I still masturbated, but something inside of me was changing. I could feel the change. This was a 90 day program, and as I worked the program, I began to see these Christians differently: they were no longer my prey; they were now my brothers. I found myself no longer going to church for stamps; I was now going to church because I wanted to be in church. I could not put my finger on the date that it happened; all I know is that it happened: I remember going to church one night, and while the praise team was up singing I noticed a keyboard sitting to their right; and suddenly, I thought to myself, "I want to get in the choir. I can play the keyboard." After church service was over, I went up to one of the choir members and I asked him how could I join the choir. He said,

"The first thing is you can't smoke cigarettes."

"Oh, forget it," I thought to myself. "That's never gonna happen." I then walked away, but there was a strong call on the inside of me to sing and play for the church. I would go to church on Sunday mornings, and when the music would began to play, I would get this warm feeling inside of me, my eyes would get teary, my heart would swell, and there was a love inside of me that was growing. I couldn't explain it. It felt like a hurricane swelling inside of me: *This is the air I breathe. This is the air I breathe. Your holy presence living in me.*

The time drew near for me to receive my award. I was finally going to receive my Bible and have my name called. I was still caught up into myself to a good degree. I was still concerned with being seen. I prided myself on accomplishing what I saw others accomplish. That is what the Bible calls the sin of covetousness, which is where you want what someone else has. I was coveting other people's accomplishments.

When it came time for me to receive my Bible, I was very happy and excited. I did it! I completed the program! That Sunday morning I could hardly contain myself. We went through the regular routines of the morning service and then the chaplain stepped into the room. I became nervous. It was time. I sat on the edge of my seat, waiting to hear my name called. "Good morning," he said. Everyone responded in kind. "Today, we have three names that have completed the discipleship program, and we have here three Bibles. I am so proud of these young men for their hard work and their accomplishment. Their names are..." He called the first name, and then he called my name: "Brother Howard!" I got up, threw my shoulders back, held my head up high, walked up to the front of the church, and received my certificate and my Bible. I then walked back to my seat feeling like a big man, having accomplished my goal. Now, everyone knew who I was. Pride entered my heart and had me wrapped around his finger. After that, I decided that I was going to join the choir. I said to myself,

"I'm going to get in that choir if it's the last thing I

do." So, I made every effort to stop smoking cigarettes. It was one of the hardest things I did. No matter how many times I tried, it seemed like I just could not stop smoking.

I began hanging around Christian brothers. When I went out on the yard, I hung around the Christian brothers. Every Friday, I was at the Christian library. Everything I did revolved around the Christians. I was determined to stop smoking cigarettes because I wanted to get in the choir. I remember being in my room one day (my prayer time was around one in the afternoon), getting ready to pray: I closed the door and put the flap over the window so that I would not be disturbed, then I got down on my knees and I began to pray (Yeah, I kind of knew God now.) While praying, I heard a soft, clear voice say to me, "Put your head to the floor." When I obeyed and put my head to the floor, I began to cry profusely. I cried out unto the Lord. I remember telling God, "God, I'm tired! I can't do it no more! I can't take it! Every time I try to fix it, I mess it up! I'm giving it to you! I'm done! I'm tired! I'm tired, God! Take it from me! Every time I try to do it, I mess it up!" I was crying from the depths of my soul. Tears were strolling down my face. Secretion was coming from my mouth and snot from my nose. As I cried unto the Lord, something inside of me took place, something that I can't explain. But once I lifted my head from the floor and I stood, I knew I was a different person, a new man. My situation had not changed, my environment was still the same; however, the old Stephen died that day and a new man was born.

CHAPTER 20:
TRANSFORMED

LOOKING AROUND MY CELL, I COULD RECOGNIZE that something happened in that room. There was a presence there which engulfed me completely. I felt whole sitting on my bunk with a warm sensation going through my body. I was revived and rejuvenated. Regeneration had taken place that day in that cell. I got up, went to my sink, pulled my face rag from the rack, turned the water on, and began to wash my face, attempting to compose myself. An unspeakable joy washed over me and I knew that God was doing something in my life. God had a plan and I was in the middle of it. After composing myself, I opened the door to my cell and walked out into the dorm. Everything was normal as if nothing happened in my room. Some of the guys were at the table playing cards and Dominos, some of the guys were in the television room watching TV, some of the guys were over in the work out area exercising, and some of the guys were in the telephone room on the phone. The officers were in their booth watching the activities of each one of us as we went about our daily routine. Some of the guys were sitting at the table reading books, some were reading Bibles; we were going about our daily routine; but I knew that something inside of me had changed... and that I would never be the same again.

Entering into the television room, I sat on the bench and began to stare at the TV, not really noticing what was on the screen. One of the guys came and sat down beside me and then pulled out a cigarette. He began to smoke it and asked if I wanted one. I said yes. He gave me the cigarette and I began to smoke. Now, a change had occurred in me, but the residue of my past still clung to my soul. Even still, I began to draw closer and closer to God. I began to read my Bible more, pray more, seek the face of God more, be in church more, play the keyboard more, go to the chaplain library more, and be around my Christian brothers more. Instead of going out onto the yard Saturday mornings to play the bingo games, I went out on the yard to be one of the attendees of the Bible. This pretty much became my routine. Every morning I'd get up, eat some chow, and then go back to my dorm and clean it up for inspection—we had to stay in the dorm until the Warden came in and inspected it, which could be three, sometimes four hours later; until then, we couldn't move. But the opportunity arose which allowed me to get out of the dorm before the Warden came: all I had to do was go to school and get my GED. I am a high school dropout. In a sense, I never completed anything in my life up until this era in my life. So this was something I wanted to do: get my high school diploma. I also wanted to go to college, but due to the choices I made in my life growing up, I ended up going in a different direction. But now that I was in prison, I had less distractions around to prevent me from pursuing my educational goal. I went to the education department and inquired about the requirements for me to receive my GED, and they told me that in order to receive my GED I had to take a placement test first, which would tell me what my level of education was. After finding out what level I was at, I began attending class every morning after breakfast to prepare for the GED test.

I quickly signed up to get my GED. Every morning after I came back from eating, I would return to my room and get it in order, grab my books, go to the door, and then yell "Education! Education!" at the officers. This would get their attention, letting them know to open the door. I would then leave out and go to school. I was determined to complete my education if I didn't complete anything else in my life. I went to school, read, studied, and asked questions. I did whatever it took to learn and get my education. My mind was only on two things: my spirituality and my education. I wasn't even worried about the ladies. The girl I was seeing before I got locked up, the one who decided to stop sending me money after I expressed to her my intention to discontinue our relationship, wrote me while I was locked up. Her letter read:

"Wow I never had anyone brake up with me while they were still in prison, this really hurts." -Val

Of course, the ink had been smeared by her tears, but I didn't want to lie to her and lead her. No longer being dependent on her for my needs while in prison, I now had to learn to depend on God. "God I am going to depend on you for everything that I need now. I don't want to depend on my brothers. I don't want to depend on my sisters. Nobody! You say that you are going to supply my needs, and I am looking to you to do just that. I am giving myself totally over to you."

As I continued to draw closer to God, things began to change in my life. I began to see things a little clearer now that the blinders on my eyes had been removed. While at church on Sundays, my heart would be lifted whenever the music began to play and I would enter into a place of worship where tears would roll down my face and I would cry out to the Lord. I was thirsty for God's presence. I was seeking that Supreme Being I had heard so much about growing up. One day, while in my room reading my Bible and preparing to lead the Bible study, I heard a voice; but this time, unlike before, it was audible. At first, it frightened me. This voice was not a booming, thunderous voice; it was soft and understandable. It was the Lord's voice calling out to me, saying, "Steve." I quickly lifted my head, looked up, and I said, "Sir?"

"If you give me all of you, I will give you all of me," the Spirit of the Lord said to me.

"If I give you all of me, you're going to give me all of you? I don't have much to give you, God. Look at my situation. What can you do with me in here? But, okay. If you want me, you can have me. I don't have much to give," I said. But then a light came on and I said, "but I have a whole lot to gain. Okay, God, I'll give you a try. I'm gonna try you out." And that's exactly what happened. That was the day my life completely changed. That was the day my life was completely transformed. I knew where I stood with the prison system, I knew that according to the law I was never getting out of prison again, I knew that I had another charge lingering over my head waiting for me, but if I gave God a try, if I just gave myself over to him completely maybe, just maybe, there was a chance for me to be with my family once again. So I asked God what must I do, and He gave me Matthew 6:33. I went out that Saturday and taught from Matthew 6:33, which reads, "...but seek ye first the kingdom of God and his righteousness and all of these things will be added unto you." God told me if I sought Him and His righteousness first, He would bless me with my heart's desires—and my heart's desire was to be reunited with my family. I said, "Okay God, I'm going to seek you like never before. I'm going to learn everything that I need to know about you. I want to get to know you even more personally. I want to have an intimate relationship with you. If you did it for my father, you can do it for me. I believe that you are a healing God. I believe that there is nothing impossible for you and I am going to give myself totally to you."

After my conversation with God and that Bible study the following Saturday, everything seemed like it was in a daze; things began to move so fast that it seemed as if I was no longer in control of what was going on in my life. God was doing some things in my life at that time that blew my mind. I began to have Bible study in my room once a week. I would have a prayer call and where many inmate would come to receive prayer. God was operating in me and transforming me into the person I was always meant to be—the person that I am today.

The biggest change came about in my life this

one particular day. I woke up and left my room, heading towards the phone room. When I got to the telephone room, I was about to call my brother. Right when I put my hand on the phone, it was like I woke up from a long dream. I dropped my hand from the phone and I looked around the room, observing my situation. "How did I get here? What happened?" I thought to myself. I felt confused, lost, wondering what was I thinking all of my life and what was I doing all this time. How did I end up here in prison? For about a month or two I literally tried to make sense of my life and figure out what caused me to spend the majority of my life in prison. It was like scales fell off of my eyes, suddenly. But on this particular day, while I was studying God's Word, I could hear Him speaking to me; He began to reveal Himself to me even more clearly.

Sometimes, when we're standing too close to a picture, we tend to overlook all of the details of it, but when we back away from it we can see the whole picture much more clearly. In a similar manner, things began to come into focus in my life; I began to see the big picture. As the Lord would deal with me, I would confide in my Christian brothers. We'd discuss these things using the Word of God—and of course, as expected, iron sharpens iron as the Bible says: we would sometimes debate what the scriptures were saying in certain passages. God would reveal to me one thing and to someone else another thing from the same verse. This is a testament to what the Bible meant when it said we all know in part because God never gives one person the full revelation. God disperses understanding and revelation to different people so that everyone will have something to contribute; no one person will have it all and know it all, and therefore, become arrogant. During these times of debating, I would search out the answers diligently by going to the chaplain library. I would randomly come across books that God revealed everything God revealed to me regarding a matter. This would occur continuously: God would lead me to books in that library that would open up to me and to others around me the revelation of His Word. I was truly beginning to understand why the Bible says in 1 Timothy to "study to show thyself approved" unto God. God speaks to us through His Word, but we must also apply ourselves to studying His Word. And when we study His Word, God will confirm His Word to us.

A hunger developed on the inside of me for truth and revelation of God's Word. I would be present at every worship service available, from the Sunday morning and Sunday evening services to the Friday night services we'd occasionally have. God was still humbling me and changing me, though. He was working on my attitude in different ways. For example, during one Sunday night service, a certain preacher came to minister to us that night, but the second he walked into the building, I began to think to myself "No way. This can't be the minister for the night." It's funny how, although saved, we still tend to judge others just from their outer appearances rather than taking notice of the goodness that is within them. This guy was a biker. He had a long beard and long hair that hung all the way down his back in a ponytail. He had on a biker vest covered with a bunch of patches, ash wash jeans, cowboy boots, a bandanna on his head, and he talked with a rough voice. I had never seen a minister look like that before. "You call yourself a man of God. You ain't no man of God," I said to myself, not knowing the gift that God had brought into the building. But when he began to talk and tell us about himself, I was taken aback; I was amazed because the very prison that now contained me was the very prison that used to hold him, the very dorm that I had occupied was the very dome that he used to live in. The words he spoke pierced my heart. I remember him saying this:

"I cried out to God and he heard my cry. That day, I gave my life over to Christ, and my whole life changed. I began to pray for the brothers. Everyone came to me for advice. I gave the Word of God. Brothers, let me tell you something: I don't supposed to be out today, but because of God, because I gave my life over to Him completely, He opened the doors for me. Now, I am able to come back and tell you that if He did it for me, He can do it for you, too. The same prosecutor that prosecuted me, I am now working with; the same police officer that locked me up, I now ride alongside with. God can do it for you, too, if you just give it all over to Him. The people that you see here with me today are members of my church. I have a church out in Canton, Georgia. God can do the same thing for you."

I said to myself after hearing this awesome testimony from this man of God, "God, if you can do it for him, you can do it for me." After the service was over, I went over to him and I said, "Excuse me, sir." He turned around, looked at me, and said,

"Yes, brother?"

"Thank you for sharing your testimony with me. If God can do that for you, He can do it for me, too."

"He sure can, brother. He sure can," the minister said, laughing.

From that day forward, I was determined to live the life that God called me to live. I knew every since I was a child that I would one day follow in my father's footsteps and become a pastor—a Bishop—and perhaps, even an Apostle. I knew that something big was waiting for me once I was released. I did not know exactly what, but I knew there was more to life for me than prison bars. I was determined that I was not going to die in this prison. I remember going to the medical center one day and noticing many of the older prisoners that had been there for 20, 30, 40 years entering into the medical department to receive their medicine; some of these guys were old men who were walking with canes; some of them could barely walk; some of them were bent over. I said to God, "God, I do not want to be like this. Please don't let me get old in prison. God, I am going to get out and do your will." I couldn't see myself wasting away in prison. My father told me something a long time ago when I was doing my own thing in the streets; he said,

"Stephen, you don't want to spend the rest of your life in prison, do you?"

"No, sir," I remember answering. At that moment, that conversation came rushing back into my mind like a Typhoon. There I was. I had changed. God knows I did. "Jesus, get me out of this prison! I am doing your will, Lord! I am reading your Word, God! I am preaching your Word, Lord. Yeah, I smoke a little bit. Yeah, I still masturbate a little bit, but I'm doing what you want me to do, God!" This was my internal plea to God. I figured I was doing good and was deserving of a blessing. I mean, I wasn't as bad as I use to be. That's how I thought. But God wanted all of me. He wanted me to trust Him completely with my life, not keep tabs on what I've done as if trying to manipulate Him into blessing me. God wanted me to release everything that was not like Him. I was still in a compromising position. Yes, I was trying to bargain with God to see what I could get away with. But I quickly remembered what the Holy Spirit spoke to me in my dorm: "If you give me all of you, I will give you all of me." There were some things in me that God still had to clean out before He could allowed me to be released.

The more I drew close to God, the more He began to clean me up. I even started to develop a distaste for cigarettes. One day, I said to God, "God, when I get out of here, I'm gonna preach your Word. I want the people to pay attention to the Word, and not smell the cigarettes on my breath and in my clothes." I realized that cigarettes would be a major distraction to my ministry, but I'm not going to lie to you and say this was an easy battle to win because this was one of the hardest addictions I had to overcome. Actually, I didn't overcome cigarettes; I was supernaturally delivered from cigarettes. I remember lying in my bunk after smoking a cigarette and I smelled my hand and it smelled bad. I would go to sleep right after smoking a cigarette and would wake up the next morning and discover that my breath would taste bad. I was always able to get a cigarette—always! The Devil knew how bad I wanted to be delivered from cigarettes, so he made it possible that I was able to get more ciga-rettes. Cigarettes began to come from all corners of the prison. It was like people would throw me cigarettes just because... But I wanted to be free from them. I wanted deliverance. I wanted to be a preacher and do the will of God.

I remember walking into my dorm room many times and dropping down to my knees and crying out to God, "God, deliver me from these cigarettes! Take them away, please God!" And after finishing that prayer, I would get up off of the floor and light up another cig-arette. It seemed like I was never going to be delivered from cigarettes. But one day, I went up to a brother's room; he was a young Christian, being very young in the faith. While standing in his door, he looked at me and he said,

"What's going on, Brother Howard?"

"Man, I don't know. It seems like I'm never going to stop smoking cigarettes."

"Didn't you ask God to deliver you from cigarettes before?" he asked.

"Yes"

"Well, God did deliver you from cigarettes. The next time you go to God, ask Him to re-cleanse you from cigarettes." I thought about it, and then said,

"You know what, Brother, you are right." Then I left his room, ran back downstairs to my room, went in and closed my door, threw the flap up over the window, dropped down to my knees, and cried out to God, "God, re-cleanse me! God, re-cleanse me, right now! God, do it now! Re-cleanse me! Take away the cigarettes! Wash me right now, God! Wash me now! Create in me a clean heart and renew a right spirit in me! God, re-cleanse me right now! In Jesus name!" After crying out to God, I got up off of my knees and I felt it—I knew that something happened. I knew that I had been changed. I went back out into the dorm and went into the television room. One of the guys was smoking a cigarette and I asked him let me get that short. He said okay. He smoked half of the cigarette and handed me the other half, which I began to smoke. Although I could sense in my room that something happened, I didn't immediately see the manifestation of that change. But I kept on reading, praying, going to church, and studying my Bible. I was determined to walk in my calling. I made up my mind that, just as Christ embraced the cross, I was going to embrace my calling. This went on for a while. You see, many people get healed and delivered when they call out to God, but many people, after crying out to God, will find themselves "being" healed or "being" delivered—this is where God is gradually taking things out of their lives and transforming them. I was being delivered.

As the months rolled by, the day was drawing closer for me to be transferred from Dodge State Prison to the county work camp in Clayton County. Summer had rolled around by then and I wanted to be baptized. I wanted to show the world that I had changed. I wanted to make a public announcement that I no longer belonged to the devil, and that I was a child of God. I had been delivered from the hands of the enemy, but I had two problems with baptism at this time: the first thing was I was hungry all of the time because I didn't have any money coming in to go to the store with. I was hungry and needed money so I could buy some soups, honey buns, drinks, Little Debbie's snack cakes, potato chips, and coffee. I had a problem going on with my flesh. And secondly, the chaplain at this prison always had a word for you when you were getting baptized. Now, mind you: I know that God is real; I heard God talking to me; and yet, I could not figure out how God was talking to this man. When whoever was getting baptized stepped into the pool, he always had a word from the Lord for them. After all that I experienced with God, I still had doubt floating around in my head. During this time, one of the guys that was at the dorm with me came up to me and said, "Brother Howard"

"Yes?"

"I know this girl. She's a big girl, but she would talk to you. She like talking to prisoners, and she pays." I looked at him and said,

"She pays?"

"Yeah. She would give you about $300 every two weeks to talk to her."

"Okay. Give me her information."

"Okay. Let me go get it and I'll bring it back to you."

"Okay."

After he left, God began to speak to me. He said, "You said that you was going to depend on me to supply all your needs. Are you really going to write this woman?" I struggled for minute, and then I said, "God, I need something to eat. You not feeding me." God said,

"Are you not eating three meals a day?"

"Yes," I answered.

"Well, I am feeding you," He said.

"But God," I responded. "I want some soup, honey buns, and some chips." The Lord then responded, "Didn't you ask me to supply your needs?"

"Yes, sir," I responded.

"Are you eating three meals a day?"

"Yes, sir."

"Well, I'm supplying your needs."

"Okay, Lord. Let me just check it out and see what will happen."

The guy returned with the woman's information and gave it to me—it was around this time I was to be baptized. The night before my baptism, I was sitting at my desk writing out a letter to this girl describing myself. I described myself as tall, handsome, muscular built, and well put together. I wrote, "I am your Romeo." Oh, I told her all type of things to make her feel good and send me some money. When I got through writing, I put the letter in an envelope, sealed the envelope, but I did not put any information on it. I placed the envelope down on the desk and then went back to my bunk and began to read my Bible, preparing to be baptized the next morning.

Sunday couldn't come quick enough. After eating breakfast, I went back to my dorm and got ready for church call. When the announcement was made, I was one of the first to walk out the door. I had my changing clothes in my hand, my Bible in my hand, and was ready to be baptized. We got to the church and the baptism pool was ready and all the guys that were getting baptized had to go in the back room to change their clothes. Once we were ready, we came back out into the sanctuary area of the building and sat in the first two rows. When the baptism service began I noticed once again everyone going up to be baptized. The chaplain would give them a word from God. I was wondering to myself, "I wonder what God is going to say to me?"

Finally, it was my turn to get dipped in the water. I got up, walked up to the baptism pool, climbed up the steps, and climb down into the pool. I was waiting for the chaplain to give me my word, and the strangest thing happened: usually, when the chaplain would give someone a word from God, he would use the microphone so that everyone could hear what the Lord had to say. But when I stepped into the pool, he pushed the mic away from his mouth, bent over, and whispered into my ear. What he said to me assured me that God was real. The word that came from God was "Leave those women alone. They are going to kill you. Leave those women alone." How in the world did this man know that I was writing a letter to this woman? He wasn't in my dorm room. He didn't hear my conversations. This man does not even come out of his office when he comes to the prison as far as I knew. How did he know? It was no one but God. When he told me those words, I looked up at him quickly and then dropped my head and nodded as if to say yes, sir. I knew God had spoken directly to me. After I got baptized, I went back to my room, got that letter, ripped it up, and threw it in the garbage can. I said, "God, I am depending on you for everything."

It was about time for me to take my GED test. I thought that I was ready to take this test, but when test time came I failed. How in the world could I have failed? I studied and I went to class every day. I paid attention to the teacher. How did I fail? I was confused. This could have been a major setback to my confidence, a major blow to what God had already accomplished in me; and yet, it wasn't. I would not allow this to keep me down. I said to myself, "Okay, you see what you got to work on, so let's get it done." My time at Dodge State Prison was growing shorter and shorter. I knew that I would be leaving soon because I put in a transfer to go to another prison; however, in order to leave Dodge State Prison, you had to be there for at least 18 months. I was knocking at the door, but God had a plan and I was right in the middle of it. One particular Sunday morning, I went to church; after receiving the word of God and after we dismissed the service, I began conversing with my friends: all of my brothers in Christ. I was telling them that I would see them later on for the night service. I went back to my dorm. I remember looking at this lady preacher on television; she was preaching out of the book of Jeremiah. I stood there, smoking a cigarette. When I got through smoking, I heard the voice of the Lord tell me to go to my room and pray. I went into my room, closed the door, put the flap up, dropped to my knees, and began to pray to God. I told God, "God, take the cigarettes away from me. I'm tired. I can't do it no more. God, please cleanse me now, in the name of Jesus." In order for me to operate in the fullness of my calling I needed this gone. After praying to God, I got up, went back out into the dorm, went into the television room, and sat down and began to look at TV. One of the guys came over to where I was sitting and began to smoke a cigarette, and he asked me if it bothered me and I said no. When he got halfway through with his cigarette, he asked me if I wanted a short, and I said, "No, bro. I'm good." Later on that day, someone else approached me with a cigarette, and I said, "No, I'm okay." I didn't want a cigarette. The

Lord cleaned me up that morning; and from that time on, I never smoked another cigarette, even to this very day. That's been years ago.

Later on that week, I was returning from GED class. I went into my understudy's room and he was looking very sad. I asked him what was wrong, and he told me that his mother was on her deathbed. "Oh man, I'm sorry," I said. "What's going on? I mean, what happened?"

"I got a letter from home and they said that mama was in the hospital on the life support machine, and that they're about to pull the plug to let her go ahead on and die," he responded. So, we stood there for a minute in silence, then I asked him if he wanted to pray. He said yes.

"Do you think God could heal her?" I asked.

"Yes," he responded.

"Now, listen," I said. "Listen very closely. I know that it can be done because I have seen it myself, but this is going to have to happen according to your faith. Jesus said 'according to your faith, be it done unto you.' Now, do you believe that Jesus can raise your mother up from the hospital? Do you believe that He can raise her from the dead? Do you believe that He can heal her?"

"Yes," he responded.

"Okay, then. Let's pray." We began to pray to the Lord for his mother's healing—that God would go into the hospital room and touch her body and lift her up. While we were praying, the Holy Spirit came into that room and I began to speak in tongues like never before. It was so intense that it hurt my belly. From the depths of my soul I cried out to God to heal this man's mother. I told God that he needed to see a miracle, that he needed to know that God is truly real. The Lord, our God, moved in that room. After we got through praying, I told him to simply believe and let me know when he got a report. He said okay. About a week later, he received a letter from home saying that his mother was back at home cooking hotdogs, walking around the house, and cleaning up. He could not believe what had happened. And from that moment on, he became a true believer. The lord God had a plan and I was in the middle of it.

CHAPTER 21:
PROMISES

THINGS BEGAN TO UNRAVEL AROUND ME AT DODGE State Prison: gang violence broke out—it was the Hispanics against the Blacks, the Whites against the Hispanics, and the Blacks against the Whites. We went out on the yard one Saturday and was called back into the prison—word had gotten out that there were weapons on the yard. It seemed that the Hispanics were aiming to kill the Blacks; so everyone was called back into the prison so that the CERT team could go out and search the yard. They had to use metal detectors because it was told to them that the Mexicans had shanks out in the yard (a shank is a knife that the prisoners would make from combs, bones, and medal strips). The shanks were buried in different parts of the yard so the Hispanic would have easy access to them once the fight broke out; but, fortunately, the CERT team found every one of them. When we were allowed to go back out on the yard, it was said to us that there was over 50 shanks hidden. Things got so bad that we could be going to breakfast, lunch, or dinner and fights between the gangs would breakout. I remember one day everyone was in the dorm waiting for the next movement to be announced so we could leave, but we had to wait until the first set of prisoners came back from wherever they were. However, on this particular day, there were two Hispanics walking down the sidewalk and two Blacks ran up behind them and "BAM!!!" They hit them from behind. The first of the Hispanic guys hit the ground so hard he began to shake. I thought he was dying. The other guy's body went limp and he hit the ground. Blood was everywhere. Witnessing this, I began to pray for them: "My God! My God! Help them! My God, help them!" I knew it was time for me to leave this place—not that I was scared or anything; it's just that I was no fool. "I got to go," I said to myself. "I got to get up out of here." I put in a transfer to be moved to another prison. In the beginning, after asking to be transferred, the counselor gave me the runaround, telling me that I had to be at Dodge State Prison for two years before I was able to go to another prison. I was furious because I knew that she was lying to me. I said "Okay. Since you don't want to give me a transfer, I'm going to write the Warden and see if I can talk to him myself. I'm getting out of here. I have done my time here, and now it's time to go." I wrote the Warden, and after a week, he called me into his office. When I got there the next day, there were eight other prisoners waiting to see him as well. I ended up being the last person to be seen. When the Warden came out of his office to call me in, he told me he was sorry for making me wait and thanked me for being so patient. After entering his office, he asked me what could he do for me and I told him that I put in for a transfer and the counselor kept giving me the runaround. I told him that I was trying to get closer to home because I hadn't seen my father since I was incarcerated. He was too old to travel this far to visit me I explained to him. He looked at my paper work and said,

"You only need to be here for eighteen months. I see you are in the GED program."

"Yes, sir," I said.

"I'm going to grant you a transfer, but I can't make you any promises. I see you're trying to go to a county camp. I want to advise you that your chances of getting there before the inmates at Jackson State Prison are slim because you are in a camp already. They are in the process of going to one, so I can't make you no promises; but I will grant you permission to be transferred." Oh my God, that was all I wanted to hear. I knew that I was about to leave this place that I called my home for eighteen months. I'd be leaving this hell hole soon. Now, I had to work on my patience. I quickly said a prayer:

"God, please give me a little patience."

I didn't know when my name was going to be called, but I knew that it was going to be called soon. My transfer was accepted and I was waiting for my name to be called on a Tuesday or Thursday; but during this time of waiting, I was placed on outside detail. I left the prison every morning going on detail, cutting grass, picking up paper, doing different things like that. When I came back in from detail duty, I went to school at night, except on those nights when we had church meetings. It is amazing to me how the Word of God, once it is applied to your life, will produce favor in your life and cause the promises of God to radiate from you and shine upon you. I say this because I remember one evening being in my dorm hearing the voice of the Lord speak to me, "Stephen, do you remember my promise to you?"

"Yes, Sir," I said.

"I am giving onto you the Joseph connection," God said.

"The Joseph connection? What is that?" I asked.

"Do you remember the story of Joseph?"

"Yes Sir. Joseph was the 11th son of Jacob's 12 sons."

"And you are the 11th of your father's 12 children. I promised Joseph a position of honor. I also promised you a position of honor."

"God, when did you do that?"

"Do you remember that day your father came to you and told you that you were going to have a great ministry, and that it was going to supersede his ministry, but you are going to go through some things?"

"Yes, Sir."

"That was Me speaking to you through your father, and I will keep My promise. Joseph was promised a position of power. I revealed unto Him his position; however, he went running his mouth to his brothers and they became jealous of him. I even showed him favor as a child with the coat of many colors, which was for kings to wear, and Joseph's brothers put him in the pit, and from the pit he was sold into slavery. But even then, I showed favor on him just as I'm showing favor on you. Joseph had to run from a woman before she got him killed, and what did I tell you the day of your baptism?"

"You told me to leave them women alone—they are going to kill me."

"And did you obey?"

CHAPTER 21: PROMISES

"Yes, Sir."

"Now, because Joseph ran, he was lied on and went to prison; however, My favor followed him. Son, you are in prison and My favor is with you. Joseph went through some hard times during his stay in prison. He even questioned Me from time to time, but he never stopped trusting Me. Joseph knew what I promised him and waited for the promise to manifest itself. You know the promise that I have given unto you. Before you knew Me, you always had hope. You hoped for the day that you would be able to go home. You hoped for the day that you could do the little things you have taken for granted. But when you allowed Me to enter into your life, I gave you the gift of faith. You are powerful, son. You will do great and mighty works for My kingdom. I will receive glory out of your life. Your brothers will not understand you, nor your sisters; but you must listen to Me and only Me. Just like I brought Joseph from the prison to the palace, so will I bring you out of this prison and to a place of praise. My son, I am giving you a prison-to-praise experience. Every promise that I have given you, I am about to perform. Everything that has been spoken over your life from your childhood until now is about to be given into your hands. You have answered the call; and because you have answered your calling, I am giving you a second chance in life. You have gained a personal relationship with Me, and I am about to give you everything that I have promised you and your parents."

Not too long after that I was in my room reading Jeremiah 30:17 and God was speaking to me. He said, "For I will restore health unto thee, and I will heal thee of thy wounds, saith the Lord; because they called thee an Outcast, saying, This is Zion, whom no man seeketh after." And after reading this verse from the book of Jeremiah, I said to God,

"God, are you saying you have restored me? Okay. Then God, I am restored, simple as that." Sometime later, I was reading Isaiah 49:8, which says, "This is what the Lord says, at just the right time I will respond to you on the day of salvation I will help you. I will protect you and give you to the people as my covenant with them, through you I will re-establish the land of Israel and assign it to its own people again." After reading this, I said unto the Lord,

"God, are you telling me you're about to reestablish everything that has been taken away from me? Okay. Then God, I'm reestablished then." I moved on those promises from God. I believed that I was restored, that my family was restored, and that everything that had been stolen from me was restored. I truly believed at that point, at that very moment, that all had been restored back to me; not only that, but I also believed at that moment that I was reestablished back in my rightful position as my father's son, as a pastor, as a leader, as a father, as a provider, as a friend, and as an asset to the community. I walked around that prison very sure of myself. I knew that I had another charge that I had to answer to, but I felt deep in my spirit that I was not going to do a lot of time in prison. Tuesday rolled around and my door popped open around 1 am. This was the day I had been waiting for. I had been at Dodge State Prison for 18 months, and it was time for me to go. I got up out of my bed, went to the door, and peeped out to see what they wanted, hoping that they tell me to pack up my bags.

CHAPTER 21: PROMISES

Then I went out to the officers' booth and they said,
"Howard." "

"Yes, sir."

"Pack it up. You are being shipped."

"Thank you, sir!"

I went back to my room, turned the light on, and began to pack my things. I told my roommate that I was leaving and that I would see him later on on the other side. He got up, gave me some dap, and laid back down. I packed my things and got out of there. Oh man, I was so glad to be leaving this prison. "Thank you Jesus!" I said. "Glory to God! I'm gone! Hallelujah! My God, I know you are good!" I left my dorm and went to the shipping area where there were two more prisoners getting shipped to another location.

After we changed our clothing we were told where we were going. I found out that night that I was going to a work camp in Clayton County. I was so happy I almost peed my pants as they say in the country. After we changed our clothes and all of our things were searched to see if we had anything that belonged to the state, it was time for us to get on the van. What really got me though was the fact that no matter where we went while incarcerated, we were always being transferred while wearing handcuffs and ankle cuffs. We were on the van going back to Jackson State Prison, and from Jackson State prison we would be given over to the next prison or county camp. This was my second time going to a county camp. I automatically assumed that this county camp would be like Troop County, County Camp. However, when we arrived at Clayton County, everything that I envisioned quickly flew out of the window. This camp had a fence that wrapped around the entire facility and stood 15 feet high with barb wire wrapped around the top. The last county camp that I went to had none of this. Immediately, I knew that I was in trouble. "Shoot, man. I might as well stayed where I was at," I thought. We got out of the van (there was about 10 of us in all) and lined up in a single file line and followed the officers into the building. Once we entered into the building, we had to strip down to our birthday suit and be searched all over again, then be re-issued new clothes, given a locker, a bunk number, boots to work in, a dorm room, and a bed number. After leaving the shake down room, I made my way to my dorm room and to my bunk and began to unpack. Looking around the dorm and observing my surroundings, I knew that I had come to a place that was much worse than the state prison. I knew this due to the fact that no one was smoking—even though I didn't smoke anymore. Just that little fact told me a whole lot. Sure, there were one or two people in the bathroom sneaking a smoke, but the fact that they were sneaking to smoke told me that this was not the county camp you would want to be at. I remember thinking, "Awe man, where have these people sent me too? Man, what am I going to do? I got to figure out a way to get up out of this place." Not realizing that God had a plan and I was right in the middle of it, I quickly adapted to my environment. My detail was an outside detail again, which was okay for a while; but I knew that winter was approaching fast and I was not the type of person that liked to be outside in the cold. Truth be told, I'm not the type of person that like to be outside when it's real hot also. The bugs, gnats, and mosquitoes I cannot stand. But I quickly adapted to my environment.

CHAPTER 21: PROMISES

I worked outside on an outside detail shoveling hot asphalt off a dump truck and into holes in the street and pot holes on the side of the road. As the road was being ripped apart by huge trucks, we had to go out and shovel hot asphalt to re-patch the streets. The sun was beaming down on me while heat from the asphalt was rising from beneath me. I was sweating profusely, and water was not helping much.

I was not allowed to have Gatorade while out in the heat working, and the only thing that I ate was peanut butter and two bologna sandwiches every day for lunch (which tasted disgusting, by the way). Nothing too major happened at Clayton County besides just a few people getting locked up and sent back to the state prison. But I had to make a move, or as the old people would say in the old days, "I got to bust a move." So I befriended some of the officers there as well as the counselor. My every intention was to get to a transitional center so that I could make some money. When I got out of prison I didn't want to have to depend on anyone. But the counselor told me that I had to be at Clayton County for 12 months. "You mean to tell me that I got to be here for a whole year before I am able to get a transfer? Maaaannn . . . Well, I might as well do what must be done so I can get out of here," I said. I asked my counselor if I could change my detail. I told him I knew how to cook, and he said he was going to check to see if I could change details and said he would get back to me before the end of the week. I thanked him and then left his office, knowing deep in my spirit that I was going to be moved into the kitchen. True enough, before the end of the week, I was called into the kitchen and, you guessed it: this was my new detail. I had to go back to my dorm and get all of my clothes and take them back to be changed out. I was given my schedule, which was breakfast. I hated breakfast because I had to get up at two in the morning, go into the kitchen and prepare breakfast for 800 inmates. I started working in the kitchen and, of course, I adjusted to my schedule. Soon, I became the head cook in the morning. I began to train the other inmates how to prepare breakfast and I also started making cinnamon rolls from scratch and other things, which had never been offered before at the camp. Oh, they loved me. I got comfortable in my position as the head cook. Not only was I the head cook in the morning, but they wanted me to come in during the afternoon and help them prepare for dinner.

Just about anything I wanted while I was at Clayton County, I was able to get—anything that was in their guidelines, that is. I didn't do anything out of the ordinary. I didn't try to break the laws or rules because I was a man of God. On Sundays, I would go to church. On Wednesdays, I went to Bible study. And on some Saturday evenings, Clayton County had night services that were called Video Church. Video Church was a service that was provided from outside churches that would record their services the Sunday before and then send their videos to the camp so we could watch their services. After Video Church was over, we would go back to the dorm and prepare for Sunday evening worship service. This was the highlight of the camp, also. While I vacationed at Clayton, I became a part of the in-house church that was held every fourth Sunday. In-house church was a church service where the inmates who were knowledgeable of the Word of God would have their turn to preach on their chosen Sundays. There were four of us who were known as the elders at the camp. Every forth Sunday of the month, one of us would bring the Word of God. I truly thank God for using me in this way because it caused me to go deeper into His Word. He said, "Seek me and you shall find me, seek me while I am near, drew nigh unto me and I'll drew nigh unto you." And I was doing just that. God was preparing me for my destiny, for greatness, to be a leader in His church. I learned more of Him and was seeking him daily. My relationship with Christ grew deep. I could not get enough of Him. Everything I longed for, I found in God. If I wasn't in the kitchen, I was buried in the Lord's Word. I was so amazed and moved at how God was using me at this time in my life. Nothing could go wrong. Or at least I believed that nothing could go wrong. In December 2010, something did go wrong. I would never forget this month and year.

CHAPTER 22:
REFUSING TO QUESTION GOD

I WAS SUMMONED TO THE COUNSELOR'S OFFICE ONE day. I went to the door and banging on it in order to get the officer's attention. Once he opened the door, I walked up the hall towards the counselor's office. While walking that hallway, I envisioned what our meeting would be about and be like. I had been praying and believing God for a miracle, and thought that perhaps this was the moment I would hear the good news that I was going home. But when I knocked on his door, I was met with an expression on his face that let me know that something wasn't right; that whatever he wanted to meet with me about, it wasn't going to be pleasant. He told me to come in and take a seat. Now, I had seen this type of facial expression before on a counselor. The last time I saw this type of look on a counselor's face, I was being hit with the news of my mother's death back in November of 2003. The look said it all, even before the counselor spoke one word. "God, not again!" I said to myself. "This can't be real! Please tell me he's not about to tell me what I think he is." Everything in me began froze. I was alert. My hands became numb cold. It felt as if a dark cloud suddenly filled the room. And then came the news: My father had just died. I felt numb. It felt as if the bottom just dropped out of my life. At first, I was in a state of disbelief and denial; but then, anger began to arise within me. The realization now that I didn't have a mother or a father set it. What was I going to do now? Who would I turn to now? "Oh God, no! Not my daddy! Please God! No! Not daddy!" That's all I could say repeatedly. "No! Oh God! No! No! Oh God, no!" I cried so until I could not shed another tear. The counselor sat there and allowed me to grieve. As soon as I composed myself, I asked the counselor if I could be allowed to go to the funeral, and his reply was

"Everyone has already tried to get you there. Your brothers called the Sheriff's department, and they said they didn't have the man power. And we cannot allow you to go to your father's funeral without one." I asked him if we could use someone from Atlanta who was a sheriff, but his answer was "No. They have to be a sheriff here in Clayton County."

There I was again, sitting in a prison while hearing the news that my parent has died and being deprived of the privilege to attend their funeral. First, my mother; now, it was my father. After sitting in a daze, in a state of disbelief for what seemed like an eternity, I finally managed to stand to my feet and head back to my dorm. Upon entering into my dorm I noticed that once again that everyone was doing that what was normal. For everyone else it was just another day in prison. But for me,

I was now in a familiar state. The memory of my mother's passing rushed back into my mind a powerful tornado wind. I was now experiencing the same feelings I felt back then: the grief, the anger, and the disappointment. It's important to note that I felt the same surge of emotions as I had before, but this time my mind was as overcome with confusion and darkness; this time, I was able to bear it more; this time, I didn't call God into question and ask Him "Why?" I was overcome with an unusual peace in the fact that I knew God had a plan for me even in this situation. But I still battled with what I knew to be true and what I was experiencing. I knew my father was in heaven and God had a plan, but I felt angry and deeply hurt by the whole situation. I sat on my bunk, still trying to process the news I had just been given. "What am I going to do now?" I wondered. I jumped up and ran to the phone to call home, but no one answered. Now I felt completely alone. I was experiencing the same emotions my siblings felt with only one difference: they had each other to lean on and I only had God to lean on; they could hug and cry on one another's shoulders, but I only had a pillow and a faith to keep me comforted. "God, you said that you will give me peace that passes all understanding. I don't understand why my father is gone, God. And I am hurting now. I need your peace in my heart God. You said that you will be my comforter—you will comfort me in my time of troubles. And God, right now, I need you to give me comfort like never before. I don't know what to do, God. Please help me understand. Please God help me!" I cried out to God.

The next morning rolled around and I had to drag myself out bed and go into the kitchen and prepare breakfast for 800 inmates. I had to pull myself together. I still had work to do: my detail. It's a cold world, a cold situation to be in. The guards didn't care, nor the other inmates; I just had to accept the fact that what was going on in my personal life was just that: my personal life. I was still expected to do my duties. I had to get right back in that kitchen and cook breakfast so that the other inmates could go out and do their work details on a full stomach. As time progressed and the pain in my heart subsided, I received a visit from my older brother. We began to talk about the passing of daddy, the things he wanted us to do, and the type of individuals he wanted us to be. I said to him, "I didn't have anybody to hold on to when daddy had died. Man, I was all by myself. Y'all had one another, but it was just me and God. Y'all cried on one another's shoulders, but it was just me and God. So I made a vow to God, Bro. I vowed that I am going to answer my call, I am accepting my call as a pastor. As a matter of fact, I am embracing my call as a pastor just like Christ embraced the cross when He was carrying the cross up Calvary Mountain. I know that being a pastor is not going to be easy. I have watched daddy cry many nights because of the saints. But I am embracing my call, man. I'm not gonna' get out of here playing no games. Man, I am so serious. I'm serious as a heart attack, man. Look, I went hard for the devil when I was out there in the world. I did some things you'll never believe, and I know that God has given me another chance. I don't have time to play now. And when I come home, I am coming over there to help you out at church until God tells me differently. And when he tells me it's time for me to go, bro, I got to go. I don't know what God's doing. I might be coming there to be the pastor. I don't know, but I got to listen to the voice of God."

My brother looked at me and said, "Well, we'll see. You got to show me, bro. Listen, I have had a lot of people come over to the church and tell me that God told them to come over here and help me with the church. I've had a lot of people say that God told them that they were to come over to the church and be under me. I have had some tell me that they are going to be the next pastor over at the church and I tell them the same thing that I'm telling you now: 'Well, we'll see.' I'm from the show me state. You got to show me. Anybody can say what they're going to do with a mouth, but you got to show me, bro. We just going to wait and see what you going to do."

"I don't know about them. I have nothing to do with that. I'm just telling you what God told me to do," I replied.

My brother visited me a few times after that, and I would tell him about how God was operating in my life. I told him about a message I delivered one fourth Sunday, and how after the service, so many of the other inmates came up to me and began to thank me for what they said was a much needed word. I shared with him how God used me to minister to others, and how afterwards, they were in tears crying out to God. To a degree, I was looking for approval from my brother, but it was only God whose approval I really needed. My life was and is in God's hands. God is the one who blessed me, even to the point of using me to form a male choir which would sing until the glory of the Lord would move in the services. I was teaching, training, and discipling men in the Lord. On the Sundays we had guests, these guys would put everything they had into their praise and God would get the glory out of their praise. My brother and I talked about a lot: church, daddy, momma, my calling in life, and what my brother wanted to do. He wanted me to come and take over the church so that he could go and travel the world and evangelize. At that time, I truly believed that this was my destiny, but God had another plan for me.

I was at Clayton County long enough, and I had my mind set on going to another transitional center. It was time for me to apply for another transfer. I figured that if I got to a transitional center, I would be able to work and make money so that once I was released I would not have to depend on anyone. My goal at that time was to get out of prison and away from Georgia, never to return to Atlanta, Decatur, and Cobb County again. I had my mind set on another city. I had no specific destination in mind. I simply felt as if God wanted me to move away from Atlanta, Georgia, and I was ready to move. I put in my transfer to go to a transitional center, hopefully back to Atlanta Transitional since I had a love for that place. I thought that place had it going on. I thought this was the best place for me. I envisioned myself back in my old position at GBA, baking cakes and pies like I use too.

It didn't take long before my transfer went through. About month or two later I was being called out to pack my bags because I was leaving and was heading back to the transitional center. I hurried and packed my bags and then went into the kitchen to eat, but was too excited to eat. There were two more inmates getting transferred: one was going to another transitional center and the other was going back to court. We all laughed and reminisced over the past and had hope for the future. I was so excited I didn't know what to do. After we got through eating, we changed our clothes and got on the van. I didn't matter that we had handcuffs on our wrist and ankle cuffs on our ankles, we were just happy that we were leaving this crazy place. We got on the van and headed back to Jackson State Prison where we had to wait on the officer from the next camp to come and get us. When we got off of the van, I asked the transferring officer what transitional center I was going too. He began to look through my paperwork. He then said, "Howard,"

"Yes, sir," I said, anticipating some good news— hoping he was going to say the Atlanta Transitional Center.

"You going to Claxton Transition."

"Where is Claxton Transitional Center?" I asked. "Man, I never heard of Claxton. Where is Claxton? Do anybody know about Claxton? Anybody? Hey, have you ever heard of Claxton?" I asked around. I wanted to know where they were sending me. "Hey, have you ever heard of Claxton? Where's Claxton located? I want to go to Atlanta. What the heck is this Claxton? Where is Claxton?" I continued. This was new to me. Finally, I ran into someone who knew where Claxton, Georgia was located; yes, they was sending me somewhere close to Savannah, Georgia, about four to five hours away from Atlanta. "Four hours away from home!" I said. At first, I thought I wanted to move away from Atlanta. With my mouth I declared that I didn't want to be in Atlanta anymore. Now, God had honored my request. The idea of being four to five hours away from home was hard for me to accept, but I learned then that you have to be careful what you ask God for because should He give it to you, you just might not like it. Still, I accepted my fate. I got on the van and I said to myself, "Okay, Stephen, you said you wanted to get away from home, so here you go." I then braced myself for the long ride, which seemingly took forever. When we finally arrived there, we got off of the van and went into building. Of course, we went through the process of changing our clothes and getting searched—you know, the usual routine. I was given a dorm room and a bunk number, and when I got to my dorm and my bunk I said to myself, "Man, you might as well have stayed in prison. This is no better than the county camp you just came from." Later on that evening, everyone was coming in from their job. I introduced myself to them, and the likewise introduced themselves to me. They began to tell me about their jobs. Apparently, everyone at this transitional center was working at the same place, which was right across the street from the center: Claxton Chicken Plant. They guys began to tell me about the Hispanic women that were waiting on the new guys to come in so they could get a man. Everyone there had a cell phone. As they began to tell me more and more about this particular transitional center, I found myself falling back to my old way of thinking. Just that quick I was falling from grace in my mind. In other words, I had relapsed in my mind. I had major plans for myself. I thought to myself, "I am going to go over there and get me one of the baddest Hispanic women I can find and then I am going to settle down here in Claxton, Georgia. I am going to start me a church down here and everything."

I called my sister and told her about Claxton, Georgia, and she said, "You know dad wanted to start a ministry down that way in Savannah, so maybe this is where you supposed to be."

"Yeah, you're right. This is where I supposed to be," I said. But deep down inside I had an ulterior motive. The next morning, I was given a detail to work in the laundry room, and while I was in the laundry room working, one of the guys came to me and asked,

"Is your name Steven Howard?"

"Yes."

"Your name is on the list to be shipped back to prison." After he said that, my heart dropped.

"What do you mean? What are you talking about?" I asked.

"I'm serious, man. It's up there at the booth. You can go and see for yourself." After the man said that, my heart began to beat real fast,

"This can't be," I said. "Just can't be" I was saying to myself while I headed to the officers' booth. And sure enough, my name was highlighted in yellow. I was scheduled to be shipped back to prison. I asked the officer, "Why do I got to be shipped back to prison? What's going on?" And he said,

"I don't know. They just put it up."

"What do you mean they just put it up?"

"Like I said, Mr. Howard. They put it up before I came on."

"What happened?" I asked.

"I don't know. I just got here. Evidently, something is going on with your paper work. Usually, if something like this happens it will be because you have another case pending with the state, and you can't be in the transitional center with an open case." I looked at the officer like he was speaking a foreign language, although I knew what he was talking about. I knew I had another case open that had finally caught up to me, and I was not happy about it. After receiving the bad news, I went back to the dorm in a daze.

"How can this be? They didn't supposed to find me," I thought to myself (it's bad when you start to believe your own lies). I found myself living an unspoken lie because I knew I had this criminal case, and yet, I was hoping and wishing that it would miraculously just go away. But God said in His Word that we shall reap what we sow. Just because I got saved and started being obedient to God, that did not mean that I did not have to answer for the crimes that I did. Once I got back to the dorm I went to my bunk and laid down and I said, "God, what are you doing? What are you doing?" I knew that God was doing something at that time, but I did not want to go through the process I needed to go through in order to receive my promise. Still, it was necessary that I do so. After lying on my bunk for what felt like an hour (but was only 20 minutes), I got up, shook myself off, and decided that I was not going to allow this mishap to remove me from God's promises over my life. God shifted me into an awesome atmosphere of faith. Every step I took was done in faith. We know that faith is the subject of things hoped for and the evidence of things unseen as declared in Hebrews chapter 11. knew how to operate in hope and faith, and therefore, I knew that regardless of what was about to happen God had my back. I knew God was doing something spectacular in my life and that it was going to be a part of my destiny. I began to relax. A sense of relief began to wash over me as if I had plunged myself into a pool of cold, refreshing water. I had an overwhelming sense of freedom within, one that led me to praise God instead of complain to God. I was free to give God every particle of my being and to live in His grace and under His anointing. I was simply glad I was able to receive the fullness of Christ and give Him all of me. "I am ready to except my fate," I said to God. "Whatever you are doing, God, I am totally trusting you."

CHAPTER 23:
HE DID THAT

I WALKED FROM MY DORM TO THE NEIGHBORING ONE and began to watch television—the TV in my dorm did not work. There I was, sitting in front of the television, minding my own business when, all of a sudden, two officers came into the dorm on a mission. They told everyone to go into the day room while they searched the entire dorm. They went from box to box, locker to locker, pillow to pillow; they went into the bathrooms to search; they searched the water fountain; basically, they searched every inch of the dorm, but they came up with nothing. After searching the dorm, the officers then came into the day room and searched everyone there, myself included. Still, they came up with nothing. Afterwards, they instructed the residents of that dorm to go to their bunks, and all the while this was taking place, I was just sitting there in front of the television. I was amazed at their attitudes. They knew something was in that dorm...as if someone had informed them that something was there that did not belong. I was sitting in my chair observing everything from the television to the officers. Then one of the officers went to the laundry basket where all the inmates put their dirty clothes, put on some white search gloves, and began to search through the dirty laundry. Then he flipped the basket upside down, separated the basket from the clothing, and all of a sudden, grass spewed out everywhere. I looked and I said, "Is that marijuana? Oh my God, that is marijuana!"

There was over a pound of marijuana, weed, pot—whatever you want to call it. It was right there. You mean to tell me that all of this was in Claxton Transitional Center, right under my nose? My God, I began to praise Him. I began to praise God for the fact that He knew that I did not belong here in Claxton Transitional Center. See, I constructed a plan to be transferred to a transitional center and God allowed it to happen, but it wasn't His plan. Did He not say, "I know the plans I have plan for you, plan of peace and not of war. A plan to give you an expected end"? God was in essence telling me "This is not your final destination. This is not where I plan for you to go, but because you wanted to move ahead of me, because you wanted to get outside of the plan, I allowed you to see where you were heading." I thanked God that I did not get reprimanded for someone else's stupidity at that transitional center. God delivered me from Claxton Transitional Center and sent me back to Dooley State Prison. This prison was known as Sweet Dooley because at Dooley State Prison you were able to do just about anything you wanted to do.

When I got there, a CERT team officer greeted us at the gate, lined us up on the side of the prison, and gave his little speech. Let me see if I can remember his word verbatim: "You are now at Dooley State Prison. Dool-

ey State Prison is known throughout the state of Georgia as Sweet Dooley because we allow you to live your
life as long as you do not bother us. When you get to
your dorm you will see that there are cell phones in your
dorm, there are some drugs in your dorm; you will find
crack cocaine, marijuana, and cigarettes in your dorm.
We will not come and search your dorm. We will leave
you alone as long as you leave us alone. We do not want
to come to your dorm because you are fighting. If we
have to come to your dorm because of a fight, we will
lock everyone down. We try to give you your space. We
try to let you live your life as comfortably as possible.
Once again, there are cell phones in your dorm. If you
are outside of your dorm and you get caught with a cell
phone, you will have to suffer the consequences. Welcome to Sweet Dooley, gentleman, and have a good stay."

I said to myself, "My God, You took me out of the
frying pan and threw me right into the fire. You mean
to tell me I am now at a state prison where they know
that you have cell phones in your dorm and they don't
care? Wow!" I was blown away. While being processed, I
was given a directive to go to G house. G house was the
dorm that everyone went to before they were moved to
their permanent location in the prison. When I got to
G house I introduced myself to a couple of people that
I recognized from other prisons. One of the guys came
over to me and said,

"Hey, man, they have this dorm on the other side
of the prison which is called the faith-based dorm."

"What is the faith based dorm?" I asked.

"Everyone is trying to get into the faith-based
dorm. This is a dorm where you can go in and practice

your belief. They have all types of people practicing their religion and belief there: the Muslims, the Christians, the wicker; everyone is free to practice their religion in the faith-based dorm." He then said, "Man, they got two televisions, they got DVD players in there, they have a microwave there, they got computers, and everything that you want is in the faith dorm. Oh yeah, check this out man: they have music equipment, too: keyboards, drums, and guitars. Everything that you want is there."

"How can I get in there?" I asked.

"Man, you got to be here for at least six weeks before you're able to even apply for this dorm."

"Well, how can I apply?"

"The paperwork is over there. But I'm telling you, man, you're going to wait at least six weeks before they even look at your paper."

"Okay," I responded. I then went over and got the paperwork and filled it out. I didn't know much about this place, but I knew that God's favor was upon me. I knew that God had brought me here for a reason (I recognized God in everything).

I filled out the paperwork; and when it was time for us to go to lunch, I put my request in the request box and waited to hear from them (that was on a Tuesday). Saturday morning, around 9:30, my name was called (yes, this was the same week): "Steven Howard! Anybody know Steven Howard?!" I heard my name being called from inside of my dorm room. I rushed to the door and I said,

"Yeah, that's me."

"Pack it up. You're moving."

"Moving? On the Saturday," I replied. So I went

back to my dorm room and began to pack my things. When I finished packing, I went downstairs and asked which dorm was I going to and the officer looked at the paperwork and said,

"You are going to E house." My mind began to swim.

"E house? But I thought I had to wait at least six weeks before I am even looked at," I said.

How was it that I was moving when no moving was done on Saturdays? God had a plan and I was right in the middle of it. God set this up. The Bible tells us of an incident where Joshua went to war and he prayed to God that the sun would not go down until he defeated his enemy and God made the sun stand still. Only after Joshua won the battle did the sun move again. With man things are impossible, but with God nothing is impossible. God told me that He was giving me the Joseph connection. So I moved from G house to E house and the guy that told me about E house was shocked. He didn't believe what he was seeing. He asked me how did I do it. I told him it was no one but God.

When I left G house, I followed the officer over to E house, observing my surroundings as I was walking. I was amazed at what God was doing. He tells us in Ephesians 3:20 that He wants to do abundantly above and beyond all that we could ever ask or think. It's according to His will that we have abundant life. And God will perform every promise that He made to you and I because, as He said, His word will not return unto Him void. I entered into E house and was amazed. This place was like no other prison that I had ever been to before. The floor was designed according to the faith of the Christians, Muslims, Wiccans, Buddhists, and every religion that you could imagine. They were all engraved on the floor of this dorm. The guys were walking around laughing, watching television, and on their phones. I really believed that this is where I belonged. Now, I can get into my Bible. God delivered me out of Claxton, Georgia, and brought me to this prison; therefore, I knew that He was doing something unusual in my life.

"God, I removed my will and let thy will be done in my life," I said. The first thing I did was head over to the music department. I opened the door to this room and there were two keyboards sitting on the stand ready for me to come and play on them. To my right was a drum set and a couple of guitars. "My God, I am in heaven" I said to myself. I quickly closed the door behind me, went to the keyboards, sat down behind them and began to play to the best of my ability. A few minutes later, JR came into the room. I was surprised to see him because the last time I seen JR was back in 1999 at Macon State Prison. This man was one of the most talented keyboardists I had ever run across in my entire life. "Hey, man," I said. He looked at me for a minute and then he recognized me.

"Hey! What's going on?" he asked. I began to explain to him what happened:

"The last time I saw you, we were at Macon State; then I got out, got back in trouble, and got arrested again. I did seven more years and was released again; and as you can see, I'm back. I got in trouble. This is my third time and, believe me, bro, this is my last time. When I get out this time, I am not coming back." After we got through catching up on the past, he got on the keyboard and began to play. I asked him to teach me to play like he played, and he said that they had a class that taught the guys who wanted to play the keyboard.

"We teach them every day to play the keyboard, the drums and guitars. If you want to learn to play, you have to sign up and we will put you on the schedule to be taught," he said.

"Okay" I said. I then left the music room, I went back to my room, and began to get ready for the next day.

Sunday came along and I went to church—and my God, this was one of the best church services I had ever been to since I was incarcerated. I mean, the praise team was on point, the choir was phenomenal, and they had these guys in their gospel groups that would blow your mind. I was amazed at the talent that was in prison. The Bible says the enemy comes only to kill, steal, and destroy, but Christ said He came so that we might have life and have it more abundantly.

As I looked around the church, I saw how the enemy was destroying the lives of these men by taking them (myself included) away from our families. But God is a restorer. God is a healer. God is a rewarder of them that diligently seek Him. You know me: I had to join the choir. I had to be a part of this great movement in this prison. It did not take me long to join the choir; and every Saturday morning, we had to be in choir rehearsal at 10 am. We learned those songs and got them ready for Sunday worship service; and when Sunday came around, we would rock the house. While there, I signed up for the GED class again. I said to myself, "Boy, you are going to get your GED if it's the last thing that you do!"

So I went to school every morning. I was determined to complete my education. I figured that if I got my GED, the doors of opportunity would be opened. Life was going pretty much at a normal pace—if you want to count being confined normal.

One day, I got a call to go to the counselor's office. When I got there, the counselor had some papers for me to sign stating that I was about to go home. Joyfully, I signed the papers; but when I left the counselor's office, I knew deep inside that I was not going anywhere because I had another case hanging over my head. As I walked back to my dorm, I looked to the sky—it was a hot, sunny, beautiful day; and I asked God (in the voice of Gary Coleman), "God, whatchu doing? I don't know what you doing, God. But I can't wait to see the results."

CHAPTER 24:
TRICK OR TREAT

WHEN I GOT BACK TO MY DORM, I WENT TO MY room and I told my roommate what had just transpired in the counselor's office. "Man, I got called to the counselor office a few minutes ago," I said. "She wanted me to come in and sign some papers to go home, but I know I'm not going home because I have another charge I got to answer to. I told her this, but she wanted me to sign the paper anyway. Then she told me, 'Let's see what happens. You never know. You might be about to go home.' So I signed them. What do you think, huh?"

"I don't know man," my roommate said.

"Think they'll let me go home? It would be nice to be able to go," I said. "But I'm not going nowhere. I got another charge hanging over my head."

"So what are you going to do?" he asked.

"I don't know. I can't do nothing but my time. What else can I do? I mean, there's nothing else to do but my time. Hopefully, they let me get out. I don't know, man. I don't know." He looked at me and said,

"Son, listen to me: I'm 68 years old. I've been here since I was 19, and have seen a lot of things during my time. I know you are a good man, and I can see that you have been going through a lot since you been incarcerated. I can see the pain in your face and I can also see how you try to cover it up. You try to mask it, but it's there. You do whatever you got to do to get out of here. Go to the law library. See if you can find a loophole that you could squeeze through to get out of here. Find a way to go home."

"The law library?"

"Yes, the library. They open every weekend. Go there and read up on your case. There is always a case that resembles yours. The only thing you have to do is go and find a case, see what they did to win the case, and you file the same paperwork. You don't need no lawyer to file a motion; they got the paperwork there. Whatever you gotta do to figure it out, do it, and send it to the clerk of court."

"Okay," I said. Just that quick, I took everything out of God's hands and sought to do things myself. I believe that if I would've left it in God's hand I would have saved myself a lot a time and energy because when I started going to the law library I never did accomplish anything. Oh, yes! I did accomplish something: I accomplished catching a headache every Saturday morning.

Monday through Friday the routine was the same: I went to GED class in the mornings, and by the time I got back to the dorm inspection was over, which was great for me since I did not want to be in the warden's face. I would come back to the dorm and everyone in the dorm would either be looking at television, playing games, looking at a movie, or on the computers. I would always run upstairs to the music room because I wanted to enhance my skill on the keyboard. Sometimes I would get there and some one would already be in the room practicing, so I would have to wait for my opportunity to go in and practice. JR never did teach me how to play the keyboard, but there was this white guy who played fairly well and was willing to teach me. He didn't know much, but he knew enough to enhance my playing skills. I would come in and he would be on the keyboard waiting for me. I believe he got joy just by teaching others what he knew. He would wait for me in the music room; and once I got there, he would tell me to take a seat. When I sat down, he would show me the cords of the keys. I began to go over the cords until it became a part of me. He was teaching me how to read the notes as well—I began to learn the notes and how to read what I was playing. This was very exciting for me because I never knew how to read music, and I knew that if I could read music as well as play music I could play for any church. But God had a plan for me that was greater than mine.

Even though E house (the faith-based dorm) was nice, it was still prison, plain and simple. Ultimately, I was ready to go home. So, one day, I just cried out to God, "Get me out of here! I promise you that I will do your will! Oh God! I promise you I'm going to do your will!" After that, something exciting happened: news spread around the dorm that we were about to have what we called "family day". Family day is a day that your family is allowed to come to the prison and spend some time with you. There were very little boundaries set. You were able to sit at the same table and hold hands, and even walk with your love ones around the prison and no one would bother you. There was going to be singing, comedy pieces, and a lot of good food. So we began to practice for family day every day. There were five singing groups. I had to help two of the groups reach a note that they could not reach on their own. We practiced and practiced; it was as if we practiced all the way into eternity. Finally, family day was upon us.

The day before the event, we had to vote to see who was going to host the show, and you guessed it: I won. I didn't try to win; I didn't want to win; but I won. Not only was I singing with two groups, but now I was also hosting family day. The next day, while preparing to host the program, the dorm representative came into the dorm and entered my room where I was and informed me that I was getting shipped back to the transitional center. Oh, the joy that leapt into my heart upon discovering that I was going back to the transitional center. That's why it was necessary for me to go fill out that paperwork at the counselor's office that day I figured. I quickly ran down to my friend who was teaching me how to play the keyboard and I told him, "Man, I'm gone, bro! I'm gone!" He asked me what was going on and I told him about the news I had just received from the dorm representative. He jumped off of his bed, came up to me, and gave me a hug, and said told me he was glad for me and also told me not to forget about him. "Believe me, bro, when I get out of here, I won't forget about you. I promise, man! Look, all you have done for me, man... You think I'm gonna forget about you? I asked JR to teach me how to play the keyboard and he acted like it was gonna kill him or something, but you taught me everything. You knew and you didn't ask me for nothing but my willingness to learn."

"Yeah, but it wasn't much," he said.

"It was enough," I replied. "Believe me, my friend, when I get to my destination and start working, I'm going to send you some money. I promise you. Look man, there aren't too many people I call my friends, especially in here." After leaving his room, I went to a couple of more associates that I was dealing with and I told them the good news.

"How do you know?" they asked.

"Because the dorm rep just told me. He said he saw my name on the transferring list a few minutes ago when he was in the office, and I will be leaving tonight!!" They all congratulated me and I thanked each one of them. "I can't believe this, man. God is good! Oh God, thank you Jesus! I am so thankful!" I said to myself. I was thanking God because I was about to go back to the transition center, or so I thought. At 1 am my door popped open and I jumped up from my bunk. I could not sleep anyway. I just tossed and turned all night long, waiting to hear my door open. When that moment came, I jumped up out of bed and went to the door. An officer was downstairs waiting for the two of us to come down so that he could inform us to pack it up. When I looked over the railing, he said,

"Howard!"

"Yes, sir!"

"Pack it up!"

"Yes sir!"

I went back to my room and finished packing my things—I had already began doing so the moment I received the good news, and also giving what little things I had accumulated away to other men in the dorm, knowing that at the transitional center I could get that stuff with no problem.

I completed packing the rest of my things and went out the door, but before I closed the door behind me, I looked back at my roommate and said to him, "You take care of yourself, old man. I got you in my prayers."

"Thank you," he uttered before turning over and going back to sleep. You see, I was leaving, but he was going to be there for the rest of his life. I went downstairs with my bags in my hands. The officer was sitting at the desk waiting for us so he could search our belongings. But I did not mind being searched this time because I was too filled with excitement over where I was going. He searched my bags, my clothes, and everything that belonged to me, and then he searched the other prisoner's bags and clothes. While he was searching our belongings, the other prisoner and I were talking about where we were going. He said he didn't know where he was going and that he believed he was going back to court because he had another crime he had committed. He believed that it was time to "face the piper" as he called it. After being searched, we left the dorm and went into the kitchen to get our breakfast. We ate and then left to go to the transferring area. This was where everything got crazy for me—it nearly caused my heart to stop beating. We left the kitchen and headed to the transferring area, but we had our mattress with us; so, on our way to the transferring area, we stopped to put our mattresses in the storage area. After we did that, we went down to the transferring area where the officers were waiting on us.

When we walked into the room, the first thing we wanted to know was where we were going. I had accepted the fact that I was going back to Claxton Transition Center even though I wanted to go to Atlanta Transitional Center. But at this point, any transition center was good enough for me. Why should I complain, right? The other inmate inquired about where was he going. The officer then looked at his paperwork and told him that he had to go back to court, which he figured. I was anticipating the best which was Atlanta, but I was accepting the worse which was Claxton. So I asked, "Where am I going, ma'am?"

"Howard?" she asked.

"Yes, ma'am," I replied.

"You are going to Johnson State prison," she answered.

My heart dropped like a bomb. "What!!!!! Johnson!! I thought I was going back to the transition center!"

"No. It says right here that you are going to Johnson State prison."

"What am I going to Johnson State Prison for? Y'all could have left me here! What am I going to Johnson State Prison for?"

"I don't know. It says something about the RSAT program. Do you know anything about that?"

"RSAT? My God, are you serious?! RSAT? Awe man, come on! You got to be kidding me!! RSAT?! Dawg gone, man! My God!"

I know that I'm jumping around a bit, but let me explain. There was a program that I went to back in 1996. I had to go to Macon State Prison, which was one of the worst prisons in the state of Georgia. When I got to Macon State, they had a program called RSAT. This program was targeting people with an addiction to drugs, alcohol, and things of that nature, and because my addiction was active back then when I got incarcerated, they decided to put me in the RSAT program. Well, I went to the program; or rather, I went through the motions in this program. After completing the program, I was released from prison. But upon my release, I quickly went back to drugs, and some 45 days later I was back in prison. So, when I got locked up the third time around, I received my grid sheet from the parole board and a part of my parole stipulation was in order to be released from prison I had to go through this program again. But I was determined not to go through this program. I did everything that I could possibly think of in order to not go through this program. I even got in the transitional center because I did not want to go through with this program. But God had a plan.

I was heading back to Johnson State Prison so that I could finish going through this program, which I hated and detested. We got on the bus and headed to Jackson State Prison so that I could be transferred to Johnson. When I got to Johnson State, everything seem to be foggy to me. I was somewhat confused. Every particle of my being wanted to buck the system. "How did this happen?" I asked myself. "My God, 12 weeks? Am I going to be able to make it through this? I don't know."

I slowly began to accept my situation. I figured that I had to do what I had to do in order to go through this program so that I would be able to get out and go home. The first week of the program was a drag: we had to get up every morning, and after breakfast, we would head back to the dorm to get ready for class (the classroom was basically a part of the dorm. We would leave the dorm area where slept, and would go to the TV room, and this was where the class was held). We basically did not go anywhere for five hours every day. We sat there in that class and talked about our drug addictions. We talked about wave crave. We talked about riding the storm and other things pertaining to drug addiction, alcoholism, gambling addiction, sex addiction, and every other kind of addiction.

After the first week, we took a test, and then the following week we talked talk about criminal addictive thinking (C.A.T). We talked about brainstorming, asserting oneself and being an aggressive person; we talked about everything that a person experiences while active in their addiction. We began to learn that addiction was a disease, and just like any other disease it had to be treated. If you have cancer, you must go and get treated for it; you have to get radiation treatment and chemotherapy. Why? Because it is a disease. Addiction is the same thing: a disease. We shared some of the things that we did while operating in our addictions. We talked about the people we hurt, and the things we did to get the drug of our choice. It was crazy! It is amazing to me how we hurt the ones that we love the most, the ones that we say we care so much about. The very ones that we hurt the most are the very same ones that would lay down their lives for us. When you're on drugs and alcohol, or have a gambling addiction or a sexual addiction, you're not only harming yourself, but you are also harming the ones closest to you: your momma, daddy, sibling(s), spouse, children, friends, coworkers, neighbors, etc. One of the most powerful and important commandments that God gave man was this: "Love your neighbor as yourself" But while we are abusing ourselves with drugs, alcohol, sex and gambling, we are also abusing our neighbors.

CHAPTER 25:
GOAL ACCOMPLISHED

As I began to think about all of the things I did and reflect on the advice shared by the counselor regarding how to handle our situations, especially should we ever relapse, I decided to take their advice. Still, I knew that my deliverance was through Christ and Him alone. See, I was fully dependent upon God. But the program did help me. But I also knew that God was real and was working in my life. As time progressed, I got a clearer understanding of my God-given purpose in life, which was to go out into the streets and this time bring hope rather than dope, bring the deliverance of God to the lost rather than bring destruction. God began to bring ideas into my mind and show me visions of my future much the same way demons use to show me visions of the houses I was to rob. I remember waking up one morning and God said to me, "Stephen, once you go home, I want you to form a program which will educate the community on protecting themselves from criminal addictive thinking people who do the very things that you have done. I want you to educate the community. I want you to go into the schools and talk to the children about what you experienced while you were out in the world. For what the devil meant for bad, I meant for good. Everything that you went through, you went through for a purpose, and I will receive glory through you. Learn everything that you must learn while you are here because once I release you back into society, I am releasing a force into the world. I am releasing a force into the world like never before. I have given you the Joseph connection."

As I listened to God, my heart began to swell and I began to cry. God was going to use me. "You are about to use me like this? Little old me? What have I done to deserve this? I just believed that you are God. I thank you for grace, God," I said through my tears. "I know you are a powerful and mighty God. I have faith in you now. God, I just believe that you are who you say you are, and I thank you for using me. Thank you, God. Thank you, God." I laid there and cried with my head under the covers, of course, because I didn't want anyone to see me crying like a big old baby. After my conversation with God, I got up and prepared myself for the day. As I continued to go through the program, I went through it with a new purpose. "Since I'm here, I might as will get back into the GED program. I might be able to get my GED while I'm here," I said to myself. So I went and signed up for the GED program and began going to class there at Johnson State Prison. I moved from the first phase of the program to the second phase. Time was moving quickly. I remember one day having an inmate-to-counselor conversation; this conversation was important because if I was not ready to be released into society after talking to the counselor, I was going to remain in prison a little longer. I remember sitting down in front of my counselor and being questioned by him. He asked me about my past. I began to tell him some things that made him shake his head in shock. "You was out there, man," he said.

"Yeah," I agreed.

I told him about my upbringing and the things that I went through due to my unwise choices, the rejection that I received from certain individuals in my family, the time my father told me that he wished I was never born because of the things that I was doing, how my father disowned me once, which encouraged me to rebel even more (not realizing that it was because of my actions my father felt the way that he felt). The counselor then asked, "Well, what is going to be different this time?" I thought about the question for a minute. I thought about my current situation: my mother was gone, and my father was gone; it was, therefore, time for me to grow up. I then looked at that counselor and told him that I had to grow up and become a man, and stop being selfish and acting like a child. I told him what Paul told me in the book of Romans: "When I was a child I thought as a child. I act as a child and I did childish things, but when I became a man I put away those childish things." I decided that it was time for me to be a man. He nodded his head in approval and said, "Okay Mr. Howard, you can go back to your dorm now." I got up and went back to my dorm feeling good about the conversation with Counselor Pete.

Time continued to fly by. I found that I was not going always hungry like I use to be, and therefore didn't feel the need to go to the store all the time. I was forced to do a lot of involuntary fasting. But I remember one day, while in the third phase of the program, some new prisoners came to the dorm. One of them was an older gentleman. We began to talk and he noticed that I was not going to the store; he, on the other hand, was getting cereal every night when they called for diet snack (diet snack was something that was given to the anemic, HIV prisoners, and others that were weak in their bodies). The diet snacks consisted of cereal and milk; sometimes, it came in the form of cheese and bread; sometimes, it came in the form of an orange or apple and a sandwich. But this old man always received cereal and milk. Every night, around seven, diet snacks were called and he would go, get it, and bring it to me. The cereal was whole-grain and it tasted like wood chips, but I appreciated it because I had nothing to eat after dinner was over (FYI: we ate dinner at five in the evening).

The older gentleman came to me and he said, "I noticed that you don't go to the store. I have money coming in and I get a diet snack every night. If you want it, you can have it, okay?"

"Thank you, I appreciate that young man," I said jokingly.

One particular evening, I didn't have anything in my box and I was sitting on my bunk studying for my GED test when they called out for the diet snack. I was expecting to receive cereal and 2% milk. I sat down on my bunk and the gentleman came to me and said, "Hey, here you go, Brother Howard." I lifted my head from my studies and I said,

"Thank you," while receiving the cereal and the

milk from him. I then put it in my locker box and went back to studying. I stopped what I was doing, picked up that little cup of cereal, and began to give God recognition for supplying me with what I needed. I looked at it and began to talk to God: "God, I may not have what I want, but you sure are supplying me with what I need." Then I put the cereal back in its place, put my head back in my books, and went back to studying for my test. Not too long after that, it was time for me to take my test. I had studied and was determined that I was going to get my GED. I was determined that this was going to be my moment. Although I was about to go home, I wasn't going to allow even that to stop me from walking through the doors of opportunity educationally. With my GED in hand, should I decide to go to college, I'd be able to and I'd also be able to get a job, one that I wouldn't be able to get without my education. I was going to get my GED, and I was going to get it…NOW!

I took the test and then left feeling good in my spirit. I knew that I passed. I had some concerns over the mathematics section, but other than that, I knew I passed this test. Time was drawing near for me to get out of prison. I was still waiting on my test results because I wanted to go home knowing that I passed. I had so much going on at that time. I was still concerned about the other charge that I had to take care of. I didn't know what was going to happen with that nor what I should do. Some of the guys I talked to about it told me to write the county and find out if they had a charge on me. With this process, I didn't know where to begin. I decided to started with Dekalb County and Fulton County—to see if I had anything pending with them. I received letter after letter saying that I had no pending charges in their counties. "My God, what am I going to do?!!?" I cried out to God. Time was growing short and other inmates were getting their dates to be released from Johnson State Prison. Some were leaving straight from the program. The very time we graduated from the program, some were scheduled to go home. I knew that I was going home; however, a pending charge could possibly keep me in prison. "God, you got to do something!" I cried. Not too long afterwards, I received a call from the front office. I was hoping that my counselor was about to tell me that I got my date and that I was going home. With hope in my spirit I rushed to the door to see what they wanted:

"Yes, sir," I said enthusiastically.

"They want you at the school," the counselor replied.

"Yes, sir," I said.

They opened the door and I walked out a little sad because I did not receive what I was looking for, which was my release paper. I walked down the walkway toward the school area still praying to go home. When I got there, my teacher was waiting on me with my test results in her hand. "Mr. Howard."

"Yes, ma'am."

"Your test scores are back."

"Oh, thank you so much," I said. She put the letter in my hand and I nervously opened it and began to read my scores. I stared in disbelief because I had never seen my test results look that way. Every part was over the 400 mark, which meant I passed my GED test. "I got my GED! Wow!" I shouted. "I passed! I passed! I got my GED!! Wow! Thank you, Lord! Thank you, God! I got my

GED!!" I did not receive my release papers to go home, but I did get my release paper from the bondage of ignorance and illiteracy, and of not completing anything in my life! "I got my GED!!!" I went back to the dorm with joy, happiness, and a sense of accomplishment in my spirit. Although I was in prison, I was able to do what I set my mind on doing. I now had that very important piece of paper under my belt.

I was now in my fourth and final phase of the program. Some of the guys were still getting their release dates to go home, but I didn't get mine, yet. One guy I talked to was telling me about what he was going to do once he finally got home. I explained to him my situation and he said, "Well, why don't you write to the City of Decatur Police Department?"

"Who should I address it too?" I asked.

"Try the Chief of Police," he responded.

"You know what, that sounds like a good idea. I had already written them, but I didn't send it. Let me write another letter. Maybe it'll work this time."

After sending a letter to the City of Decatur, about two weeks later I received a slip stating that I was to report to the warden's office on the next day. "What am I going to the warden's office for?" I wondered. Of course, that night, I could not sleep because I was anticipating what might be awaiting me the next day. When the next day came, I went to the door, pushed the buzzer, and said, "Administrative office, please! Open the door!" After the officer let me out, went to the administrative office. While walking that hallway to the warden's office, I said a quick prayer: "God, I don't know what I am about to face. I don't know why the warden called me up to his office. But you are in control of this situation. Thank you, Lord." When I got to the warden's office, Sergeant Jennifer Ross of the City of Decatur Police Department's burglary division was waiting for me.

"Mr. Howard?" she asked.

"Yes."

"I'm Sergeant Ross from Decatur. You wrote us and I am glad that you did because if you would not have written us, once you got out, we would have rearrested you," she said.

"Okay. Well, I'm glad I wrote you, too," I replied.

"Is there a place that we can go and talk?" she asked one of the officers.

"Yes, ma'am," one of the officers replied. He then led us to the warden's conference room and closed the door behind us. Sergeant Rose reached into her bag and pulled out a folder. She pulled out of that folder some pictures, which she then laid on the table face before me. I could see the person in the pictures. She slid the pictures towards me and asked me if I recognized the person in the photos. I looked at the pictures and suddenly started to cry.

"That's not me! That's not me! Oh God, that's not me!" I cried. She looked at me with compassion in her eyes, and then asked,

"Do you want to tell me all about it?"

I nodded my head yes and proceeded to tell her about my addiction problem. I told her how long I had been on drugs and alcohol and the battles I fought daily. I told her about the things I did that I really didn't want to do nor was I proud of doing. I was like the Apostle Paul who stated in Romans 7:15,

"...for that which I do I allowed not, for what I would, that do I not, but what I hate, that I do, if then I do that which I would not, I consent onto the law that it is good, now then it is no more I that do it, but sin that dwelleth in me, for I know that in me, that is, in my flesh, dwelleth no good thing, for to will is present with me, but how to perform that which is good I find not, for the good that I would I do not, but the evil which I would not, that I do, now if I do that I would not, it is no more I that do it, but sin that dwelleth in me I find then a law, that, when I would do good evil is present with me, for I delight in the law of God after the inward man, but I see another law in my members, warring against the law of my mind, and bringing me into captivity to the law of sin, which is in my members. O wretched man that I am, who shall deliver me from the body of this death, I thank God through Jesus Christ our Lord. So then with my mind I myself served the law of God, but with the flesh the law of sin."

After she showed me the pictures, I told her about that night. "The night I did this burglary, I used this lady's identity to buy cigarettes to sell," I told her. I told her everything that I could think of from that night, and then I began to tell her how my life has changed since being incarcerated—the direction that I was going in and what I wanted to do once I got out of the program, and hopefully prison. I told her that my intention was to go to the school and talk to the children about drugs and alcohol.

I began to tell her about the change that God performed in my life and how I just received my GED. "I want to make a difference not only in my life, but in society," I told her. "I do not want to be a liability to the community. I want to be an asset to the community. I want to help the community and, if I got one more chance, I am going to do just that."

"Well, I understand that you have changed, Mr. Howard, but we must go through the process and I cannot promise you anything. I understand about addiction: my brother died from addiction. So I try to help as many people as I can. I understand that you don't want to do this. It hurt my whole family when my brother died from drugs. So, anything that I can do to help you, Mr. Howard, I would do. I really believe that you are trying to change. So tell me what are you looking for?" she asked. "What do you want from us?"

"If I could get everything ran concurrently with what I have going on now, it would be great. If they could give me five years ran concurrent, hopefully, then I can go home," I said.

"Once again, Mr. Howard, I cannot make any promises, but let me see what I can do. I have to speak with the DA and see what they want to do."

"Yes, ma'am."

When we got up to leave the conference room, she shook my hand and said, "I believe you going to be alright, Mr. Howard. You will hear from me in about a week or two."

"Yes, ma'am," I replied.

When I left the presence of Sergeant Ross, I was filled with hope. I went back to my dorm and began telling everyone about the conversation I had with Sergeant Ross. I believed that everything was going to be alright. I had been through so much during this time in my life. I said to God, "God, please! Please, Lord! Allow me to go home."

Two weeks passed. It was around 12 in the afternoon on a Tuesday when my name was suddenly called to report to the officers' booth. I was instructed to go to the mail room. "The mailroom? This time of day?" I thought to myself. As I left out of the dorm and headed up the walkway, I began to pray a little prayer: "God, I don't know what's going on, but you are in control, in Jesus name, amen." Once I reached the mailroom, I waited in line until my name was called. When I stepped up to the window, the lady asked me my name. I told her my name. She brought a letter to the window, which I had to sign my name in order to receive. When I received the letter, the address was from the City of Decatur Police Department's criminal investigation division. I said another quick prayer before opening the letter. When I read the address and opened the letter, I read these words:

"Mr. Howard I spoke to the victim of the burglary case Mr. and Mrs. Dawson and told them about the conversation you and I had last week and explained the situation regarding the outstanding warrant for their case that you have never been formerly arrested for due to your incarceration since 2008. I let them read your letter to me the memo from Constance Johnson and the program outline you sent to me they agree that the best solution is to close the case without pursuing the war-

rant so that you could go forward with the release program this mean the case ends now, without an arrest or transfer and without the case being sent to the district attorney's office I have canceled the warrant and notified the Department of correction to release our hold. This is a gift Mr. Howard. Consider it a gift to celebrate the, the start of the new life you told me you wanted. In the 15 years I have been a police officer I have been lied to and played too many times to count. I try very hard not to lose belief in people just because so many have let me down and some days that is very, very hard to do. I believe you want to be a success and I believe you can be. Anyone can be a success if they refuse to give up and turn to substance abuse and crime. That's not to say there won't be hard days, disappointment, and frustration because there will be. Everyone has to deal with those things. It is how you deal with them that make you who you are. I wish you luck, strength, and hope you and your son build a life together from here on. Keep in touch if you feel comfortable doing so."
—Sergeant Jennifer Ross.

When I read the letter, I was speechless. Walking back to my dorm, I read it over and over and over again. I must have read that letter about four times before I walked through the door of my dorm. When I entered the dorm, everyone saw the expression on my face and began to wonder what was going on. Not only was I reading this letter as I walked, but I was crying and praising God with tears strolling down my face. I could not

believe that I was about to go home. "God, you have answered my prayer. You are really bringing me from prison to praise." I allowed some of the other guys to read the
letter. One of the guys was an old man—when he read
the letter, he looked at me and said,

"Howard, I have been in prison for over 30 years
and I have never seen anything like this."

After receiving this letter, time went by so fast it
was unbelievable. I graduated from the program. Some
of the graduates received their release papers that day.
But I was still waiting on mine. The following Tuesday, I
was instructed around 1 am by an officer: "Pack it up!"

"Pack it up? Where am I going?" I asked.

"You are going back to Dooley State Prison" the
officer responded.

"Are you serious?" I asked. I knew that if I did
not receive my paper from the parole board, my name
was going to be on the list to go back to prison. I wasn't
the only one going back to the prison that I came from;
60 of us were being transferred back to the prison we
came from that morning. I packed my things and was
transferred back to Dooley. When I got there, I did not
go back to E house because I was not going to be there
long. They put me in F house that Tuesday, and on that
Friday I was summoned to the counselor's office. When I
got there, the counselor gave me a letter from the parole
board, which read:

"Mr. Howard after reviewing you case and your
completion of the recommended program you are
to be released January 3, 2012, you are required
to report to your parole officer once you are re-

leased."

This was given to me the month of December 23, 2011.

I went back to my dorm with tears in my eyes. "This cannot be happening! I am about to go home in a couple of weeks!" I thought. When I got back to my dorm, I shared the good news with one of the guys that came back with me from the program. He almost went crazy because he did not receive his paper yet. I said to him, "Just hold on. It's coming." Four days prior to me going home, I went to the hole (like a holding protection cell). This was necessary because whenever an inmate is about to go home, they lock them down for their own safety. For me, however, it was around New Year's and most of the officers were not going to be on duty because of the holidays; so I had to be locked down for four days. When I entered into the cell, I entered with peace in my heart. I was in that cell by myself for three days, which I took as time to meditate on the Lord. I told God, "God, once I get out of here, I am going hard for you. I am not turning around and I am not playing no more. It's all about You now! Thank you Lord for one more chance!"

On January the 3rd, at 9:00am, the door to my cell opened. I walked out of that cell and went to the intake/ outtake room. I changed out of my prison clothes and into a pair of brown khaki pants, a white shirt, a pair of cheap tennis shoes, and a blue coat. It was cold outside, but that didn't matter to me. With my ticket in my hand and a check for $25, the officer transported me to the bus station. When the Greyhound bus arrived, I proudly stepped onto the bus—this time, there were no handcuffs around my wrists and no ankle cuffs around my ankles; I would not be heading to an intake room to be processed and given a speech by a C.E.R.T officer; I would not be assigned a work detail. This time, I was going home. It was at that moment that I can truly say,

"There is a praise on the inside that I can't keep to myself." This was a genuine from-prison-to-praise experience. I had been set free from every prison I was bound in from the physical, to mental and emotional, and most of all, the spiritual prison. HALLELUJAH!!!

ABOUT THE AUTHOR

A life of drugs and crime took him down the path of prison. After spending 23 years behind prison bars, Stephen O. Howard has a wealth of knowledge about the streets, but he also knows first hand what the supernatural power of God can do in a person's life. God changed his life completely.

Stephen is the founder and pastor of True Visions Global Christian Ministry. He is married to LaTasha R. Howard, and the father of 5 (Stephen, Corey, Richard, Rahkem, ConQhetta, Reshina, Brittany and Nedra), and grandfather of 18.

CPSIA information can be obtained at www.ICGtesting.com
Printed in the USA
LVOW11s0900080416

482741LV00001B/1/P